THEATRE-IN-EDUCATION

Four Secondary Programmes

Edited and Introduced by
PAM SCHWEITZER

Eyre Methuen
London

First published in Great Britain in 1980
by Eyre Methuen Ltd
11 New Fetter Lane, London EC4P 4EE

'General Introduction' and 'Theatre in Education at Secondary Level'
© 1980 by Pam Schweitzer

No Pasaran © 1980 by the M6 Theatre Company, Rochdale
Example © 1980 by the Belgrade Coventry Theatre in Education
Company
Holland New Town © 1980 by the M6 Theatre Company, Rochdale
Factory © 1980 by Rosemary Linnell

Set 8/9 pt. Press Roman by 🄰 Tek-Art, Croydon, Surrey.
Printed in Great Britain by Whitstable Litho Ltd.
Whitstable, Kent

ISBN 0 413 40180 4

All rights whatsoever in these plays are strictly reserved and application
for performance etc. should be made as follows. No performance may be
given unless a licence has been obtained.

No Pasaran and *Holland New Town*
The M6 Theatre Company,
Oulder Hill Theatre,
Rochdale,
Lancs.

Example
The Administrator,
Theatre in Education,
Belgrade Theatre,
Coventry CV 1GS.

Factory
Rosemary Linnell,
The Curtain Theatre,
26 Commercial Street,
London E1 6LP

Contents

General Introduction

A New Concept in Publishing

Of all theatre forms, Theatre-in-Education is perhaps the most difficult to convey in print. It is essentially a collaboration between a professional theatre company and a group of children. What the actors say and do is reproduced here. The children's contribution is not. It is described in general terms, and those who have seen T.I.E. in schools may be able to interpret these descriptions fairly accurately. But for those who have never seen the work in its intended setting, a great imaginative effort will be required in order to sense the real programmes beneath the texts.

Some T.I.E. programmes travel and print better than others, and it would have been tempting to have featured in this series those performance-based shows where the children are audience rather than participants, and where all the dialogue is for the actors. Some of the strongest of such programmes are included in this series as they represent an important aspect of T.I.E. companies' work, and they will probably read more easily than the rest. However, the need seemed to be to find a way of printing the participatory shows which are the stock in trade of T.I.E. companies, but of which so little is known. Companies fight shy of presenting them at conferences and festivals because it is so difficult to reproduce the conditions and atmosphere for which they were created. The lecture-demonstration has emerged as a means of conveying the essence of a participatory show, but this has its drawbacks in that the tension of the piece has constantly to be broken in order to explain what would normally happen with the children at this or that point. It becomes an academic exercise rather than an emotional/aesthetic experience for its audience – valid but different.

Few companies have even attempted to record their participatory programmes to date, and it is hoped that this series will encourage them to do so in future, so that good ideas do not disappear without trace. As it is, there is a high proportion of Coventry T.I.E. scripts in these volumes, as that company has been most scrupulous about recording its many successful shows.

Most of the programmes featured here were devised for single classes of school children in provincial schools, unglamorous venues where never a theatre critic is seen. Yet in these provincial classrooms, new theatre forms are being tried, new programme structures and new teaching methods are emerging which are of considerable significance to the otherwise very separate worlds of education and theatre.

Education

Learning Through Experience

At the heart of T.I.E. in educational terms is its concern with learning through experience. It is part and parcel of the progressive view of education which sees the learning process as a two-way affair in which the child's commitment to the activity is as significant as the teacher's programming, and considers that this commitment is most likely to be forthcoming where the child sees connections between what he is learning about and what he already knows. Much of what happens in a T.I.E. programme looks towards the child thinking, 'I didn't know I knew that, but now I know I did and do.' Playing on what every child has, a strong curiosity about strangers, some understanding about human relationships and a love for a good story, the actor engages the child's interest in a subject, gives him the detail which brings it to life, and then puts him in a situation where he has to use that interest and detail to some avail – to help someone, to solve a mystery, to make decisions and choices.

Language Development

An important part of the T.I.E. process is the recognition by the child that he is in possession of key facts and ideas which no one else in the plot can provide, and which he must articulate for the plot to progress. 'Language development' is high on the list of educational priorities, but planning for it in a school does not guarantee that it occurs. T.I.E. attempts to engage the feelings of the children by involving them in the lives and difficulties of the characters they meet, and it is through their emotional involvement that their language flow is released. There is a pressing reason to talk in the heightened situation, and such pressing reasons are hard for the classroom teacher to create in the normal run of events. Once the child has spoken for himself the new ideas, dilemmas, concepts, once he has applied them in the T.I.E. programme, they are part of his experience and can be recalled and used by him in related situations outside the programme in his own life.

Key Issues Tackled

This learning opportunity is not one to waste, and so T.I.E. teams tend to choose topics for their programmes which they consider significant for them and for their young audiences. They must open up areas which the teacher would find difficult, either through lack of research time or, less obviously, through lack of confidence about raising complex moral, social and political issues with their classes. There is still a general feeling that children should not have to worry about such things, which in any case would bore them and which they would not understand. T.I.E. teams have certainly found ways of disproving this bland assumption by offering programmes within which quite young children tangle enthusiastically with 'adult' problems when transmitted through absorbing plot and convincing, engaging character.

Because the children identify with certain characters they learn from and with those characters. Then, by having what they have learned tested and challenged by other characters, they are able to sharpen their knowledge and possess it more fully. It is a personal experience which can remain with them long after the event and, equally importantly, it is an experience which all the children have shared. The teacher can use it as a common reference point, a set of clearly understood particulars from which all members of the class can approach more general realisations in later work.

Follow-up

It has not been possible to include in these volumes the follow-up material devised by companies for use by teachers, but this is often extensive and highly imaginative. Anyone attempting to mount any of the T.I.E. programmes in the series can receive details of the accompanying teaching schemes from the originating company. Together with a good programme, a follow-up pack can form the basis of anything up to a term's work for the classroom teacher, especially for one who has seen other T.I.E. work and knows how to capitalise on the rush of interest and enthusiasm it generates so that it can be ploughed into other related constructive activity. Few teachers have the chance to see T.I.E. regularly, as there are so few teams, and those there are have to cover large numbers of schools and several age groups. It is hoped that the collection of scripts in this series will help interested teachers to recognise classic T.I.E. structures and methods, so that they can utilise programmes more fully, and can be more constructively critical of the theatre events which do come into their schools.

Theatre
A Means not an End

T.I.E. companies are not in the business of converting young people to the theatre experience per se and, in all the programmes in these volumes, theatre is essentially a vehicle rather than an end in itself. It is a means of communication with a group of youngsters, and the content of the communication is of prime importance. Gone are the days when actors worked with children's theatre companies in order to earn an Equity ticket which would give them access to the 'real' theatre, and did not concern themselves overmuch with the shows they had to perform. The massive acts of condescension underlying much children's theatre, which led to its concentration on illogical fantasy, extreme dottiness and exaggeration of characterisation, purposeless terror, silly pranks and token participation on an hysterical plane, have been held up to question by T.I.E. companies. In order to demonstrate that seven-year-olds can rise to an intellectual challenge and participate in debate on issues which the company themselves think are important and exciting, T.I.E. teams have pioneered innovatory forms of programme devising, staging and actor-audience relationships which might well prove significant for other branches of the theatre.

Group Devising

All the programmes featured in this series were devised by the whole company; that is actor-teachers, designers, musicians, as well as directors and writer-researchers. Although it is often the enthusiasm of one team member which puts a prospective show on the company's drawing-board, it is only if it interests all the group that it will get any further. This tends to ensure that, whatever the initial dramatic incident or story may be, there is likely to be a topic of long-term interest and wide significance underlying it which it can serve to illustrate. More commonly, the theme is determined in advance, and the particular story or image which will illustrate it has to be found during the research and discussion stage. This is why companies are now looking for new members with devising abilities who can translate an idea into a theatrical event which will engage the children. A lot of creative thinking goes into bridging the gap between the decision to do a show on, say, local government, and the one-and-a-half-day thriller for twenty fifteen-year-old pupils (Holland New Town) which is the end result. And the distance between deciding to demystify for infants how the West was won, and the arrival in the school hall of a caged Indian, is marked by a long hard period of research, discussion, improvisation and preliminary structuring in which all members of the company take equal responsibility. Most T.I.E. workers find this democratic way of working stimulating and rewarding, in spite of the obvious personal and aesthetic difficulties inherent in it, and companies who operate in this way tend to keep their personnel longer as each member has a stake in the end product.

A Two-way Process

However, a show which is commendably committed, consistent and coherent, but which fails to engage its audience might just as well never have been devised. An alienated young audience has obvious and unnerving ways of demonstrating its lack of involvement. T.I.E. being essentially a two-way process, new forms of actor-audience relationship have had to be invented which will allow a company to test whether and how far a genuine communication has taken place. Companies have found, for instance, that younger children particularly engage more speedily with the ideas at the heart of the programme if they meet one character at a time, rather than several who talk to each other in the children's presence. If that one character talks to them directly, and elicits replies and ideas from them about what he has said, it helps them to understand, and show him that they understand, his attitudes and problems clearly. Then they can be presented with other characters who view things quite differently, and the resulting conflict prevents them from viewing simplistically situations which are morally and socially complex. Plots can then often be built around the need for the children to represent the views of one character to another, or to make a judgement between conflicting characters on the basis of the evidence they have been shown.

Pre-determined Structure

However, this audience involvement is in no way similar to that implied in a 'happening.' T.I.E. companies do not intend to provide a stimulus merely in order to provoke a response for its own sake. There is nothing random about the audience's reaction, although of course no two audiences will express their feelings in quite the same way. Nor is it like involvement in a drama lesson, where the class assumes a major responsibility for what follows the initial stimulus, where the teacher often takes a determinedly low-key role, and where the event is truly open-ended. And in T.I.E. of course there is no question of tailoring a programme completely to the needs of a particular class, as the drama teacher can and must. The T.I.E. show must work for many groups and, although the actors need to be highly sensitive to the reactions of each audience, they must stay with the play to its conclusion. Like any other play, the T.I.E. programme manipulates the audience's emotional response throughout the event, aiming for particular effects at particular times — moments of tension, fear, empathy and release which are crucial to its success.

No, the children's participation is part of a tight programme structure and, although what they say and do can affect outcome, this is within clearly defined limits. At key points, having encountered characters, witnessed conflicts and shared in crises, the children choose between two or three courses of action, and the company switch to Alternative Plot 1, 2 or 3 accordingly. It is an important part of their decision-making process that the children see the consequences of their choice; power implies responsibility, and individual characters often round on the children and challenge the wisdom of their decision. Then it is up to them to defend it.

'Adventure' as a Form

Because of this unusually close and reciprocal actor-audience relationship, and because of the obvious impossibility of reproducing conventional theatre staging in the school hall, new presentational forms have been pioneered by T.I.E. teams which owe something to street theatre, but perhaps more to the adventure trail. The action is not confined to one space, but occurs wherever actors and children meet, often way outside the school boundaries and sometimes apparently accidentally. Like a group of detectives on the trail, alert to every nuance of the characters, the children divide up to pursue clues and then report back new findings to each other. It is up to them to see the connections between the events they have witnessed and discover the plot beneath. These 'adventure programmes', as they have come to be known, are the most difficult of all to present in the written form, especially as they often entail several events happening simultaneously, and they have presented the biggest problem in the compilation of this series.* Indeed one or two particularly exciting scripts have had to be abandoned, as companies have not felt it was possible to do justice to them without the use of accompanying videotapes and commentary. However, the excitement generated on this sort of trail is extraordinarily powerful to witness, and is a genuinely new use of theatre skills in the service of important ideas and fundamental issues. It is to be hoped that this series is a first step towards ensuring that the progress made by T.I.E. teams in pioneering such new and effective theatre forms for children can be more widely recognised and emulated.

Holland New Town, Travellers and *Ifans' Valley* are all, in their different ways, examples of this 'adventure' format, the first being the most difficult to follow, but perhaps the most exciting of all.

Theatre in Education at Secondary Level

The Writer's Role

No Pasaran and *Example* are the first published plays which are the result of a collaboration between Theatre-in-Education Companies and writers, and so it is worth saying a little about the role of the writer in this field. With a few notable exceptions, relations between writers and T.I.E. companies have been vexed and somewhat unsatisfactory in the past, and there are some obvious problems to overcome. Unless the writer has previously worked with the company as an actor-teacher, he is an outsider, joining a tightly-knit group who have their own devising methods and who are used to taking full responsibility for programme content and design as well as performance. Shedding a large measure of this responsibility to an 'expert' writer is, in the eyes of some teams, contrary to the collective creation principle which underlies T.I.E.

For the writer too, there are tremendous difficulties. His work is under constant surveillance and is modified at will by the company. Over his shoulder as he writes, he can sense this and that reservation about his ideas and can easily lose confidence, if not patience. His proposed scenario may be deemed unworkable before he has a chance to prove the contrary, or, if it is accepted, he may find that the actual writing has to be crammed into a rushed devising/improvising schedule which limits what he can achieve with even the best material. If he works from the company's improvisation, an ideal source in many ways, he may run the risk of becoming a mere scribe, whose own artistic freedom is intolerably restricted.

However, in spite of these problems, writers are still interested in writing for T.I.E. companies and they clearly have an important role to play, especially in relation to secondary school programmes where many companies prefer performance over participatory formats. The writer can construct a far more ambitious plot than can a company who are working through the necessarily hit and miss improvisation process. He can ensure that there is variety of pace and intensity and that climaxes are properly prepared for. He can brighten and tighten dialogue and, above all, he can cut. There is a tendency in T.I.E. shows to reproduce life, longueurs and all, and the writer's editing function is most beneficial. The key requirements appear to be trust by the company in the writer's ability, and respect on the part of the writer for the company's opinions and skills.

The two plays scripted by writers in this volume were actually the result of a group devising process, and in the introductions to *No Pasaran* and *Example* more is said of how the collaboration worked in practice. In fact all four programmes featured here arose out of a need felt by members of the companies to tackle the particular issues concerned. A wave of public interest might have been the springboard for the programmes, but all are also topics of long-term interest and concern. In this, they are typical secondary T.I.E. programmes; they are about subjects which are important, if difficult, to tackle at any time, but are particularly relevant now. T.I.E. is an educational and theatrical medium which can respond quickly and effectively to events and bring them before children when they matter, in a way which will demonstrate why they matter.

Political Education

There is currently great interest in the idea of introducing an element of political education into our secondary schools, following the shocking revelations of pupils' ignorance of the whole field as revealed in the Hansard Society's report, 'Political Awareness of the School-leaver'. Latest thinking on political education, as expressed in 'Political Education and Political Literacy' (Longmans 1978) is that it should not consist of teaching pupils British Constitution, much less lists of names and dates, but rather the broad concepts underlying current political debates which will affect them directly in their lives:

'To have achieved political literacy is to have learnt what political disputes are about, what beliefs the main contestants have of them, how they are likely to affect you and me. It also means that we are likely to be predisposed to try to do something about the issue in question in a manner which is at once effective and respectful of the sincerity of other people and what they believe.' (p. 13)

Professor Bernard Crick, joint editor of the above mentioned report, has given specific recognition to T.I.E. as an effective means of conveying key concepts, since a play can offer 'an empathetic grasp of different viewpoints as strong as they come'. *(Times Educational Supplement* 9.12.77.) In T.I.E., the viewpoint is part of the character, and what a man thinks about an important matter can be linked to what he does, and is therefore seen to be an important part of what he is. In this sense political attitudes are realised, given meaning through character and action.

But a T.I.E. team does not simply want to give an airing to all points of view on a particular issue and leave it at that. Empathy is not to be distributed equally to all the characters, and FAIRNESS is not the key principle which it is in Professor Crick's report. Shows are devised to add up to a statement which reflects the team's perspective. Of course many views must be put, and the show must let all the characters have their say without tipping over into the agitprop techniques of pitting characters (goodies) against caricatures (baddies). But T.I.E. is an art form as well as an educational tool and the artist must not only state, but move towards resolving, moral and political dilemmas; not didactically, but through careful manipulation of the audience's sympathy for particular characters at particular moments. So, in *Example,* the audience must understand the climate in which Lord Goddard was judging, and the reasoning behind making Bentley the 'example' in question, but it is crucial that the audience response to Bentley's hanging is one of sadness and anger, not the feeling that a good day's work was achieved by the British legal system. This was the response of the team themselves, and their priority is to enable the pupils to see how they came to feel this.

Of course there are programmes where there is no 'company line,' and *Factory* is a case in point. Positions are clearly differentiated, battle lines between management and workers, in this instance, are drawn up, but no judgements are made by the company. The pupils themselves are such active agents in this programme that, as Rosemary Linnell, the director, points out in her introduction, 'It is very important that... the actors can be confident enough and sensitive enough to play a supporting part without ever forcing an issue or determining the outcome, either for their own satisfaction or in order to supply a "right answer".' But the value of *Factory* as political education is not in doubt, and few of the pupils who have taken part in the negotiations for a contract acceptable to shop floor and management in this highly realistic setting will treat the words 'industrial dispute' as a cue to turn the television off in future.

Much energy is currently going into combatting racism in schools, but teachers are only too aware that a lot of what they say, partly because it is they who are saying it, in no way strengthens their call for a non-racist society. What a play like *No Pasaran* can do, which a teacher cannot, is to catch the pupils unawares by showing them appalling events from which they appear to be safely distanced and to which they can therefore respond openly and sympathetically, and then suddenly close the gap and bring them up against a known situation. The switch from Germany to Britain between Parts 1 and 2 of the play is a highly effective shock tactic designed to knock home with all force the connection between a Nazi Germany and a possible fascist Britain.

Holland New Town hits below the belt too, by lulling the pupils into a false sense of calm, even of boredom, on their Town Planning Course, while a web of intrigue is woven by the powerful citizens and officers around them, so mirroring exactly the process they, when they are adults, are in danger of falling into as passive rate-payers who do not question the way their local community is run, or, if they do, feel powerless to do anything about it. Their identification with the caretaker is thrown back in their faces when they see him standing impotently by as the planner sweeps the model of his carefully improved little house on the floor to make way for a fly-over. It is through their vain efforts to get him to take an initiative in his own interests that they realise they must operate differently themselves.

Pupil Involvement

Theatre companies are often nervous about involving upper secondary pupils actively in their shows on the assumption that there will be automatic resistance stemming from embarrassment and physical inhibition. They prefer to limit participatory work to infants and juniors where the take-up is so obviously enthusiastic. And certainly much of the strongest work for the secondary age range is in the form of straight plays which involve the pupils vicariously rather than through direct participation. *Sweetie Pie*, an earlier Methuen Young Drama playscript by the Bolton Octagon T.I.E. Company, *No Pasaran* and *Example* have played also to wider audiences as a result of their effectiveness as straight theatre. They do not need an educational context and this can be an important consideration for T.I.E. teams, who sometimes want to reach out beyond the schools.

However, in both *Holland New Town* and *Factory*, the pupils have proved willing to take the plunge and have benefitted greatly from their active involvement. In both cases, they have been helped by the emphasis on reality, by the provision of an elaborately realistic setting, and very straightforward, low-key performances by the actor-teachers. The pupils have been asked to respond to situations and to perform actual tasks, rather than to act or pretend. The operations they have been asked to perform have been well within their capacities and have been, in a manner of speaking, 'cover operations'. Siting local amenities on a plan and going through the agenda of a typical council meeting *(Holland New Town)* or choosing colours for a new product and learning how to assemble it *(Factory)* may be useful activities in their own right but, in both cases, it is the angle put on these activities by the characters and the fictitious situations which makes them a significant part of the learning process. In the former programme, their importance lies in the fact that they allow the pupils to observe with impunity the conflicts between their instructors, and in the latter, they enable the pupils to identify with a particular position and to take one side rather than the other in the ensuing conflict. T.I.E. is not for teaching skills, but for working out relationships, seeing connections, understanding the complexities of social hierarchies, seeing through specious arguments and divining truth.

In the case of *Holland New Town,* the pupils are in a 'witness' relationship with the plot material; that is, they have no axe to grind personally, but judge the characters and situations impartially on the evidence they are shown. There are no direct emotional appeals to them (although of course the plot and the characterisation are tilted against the planner) and the pupils' involvement is allowed to remain ostensibly low-key throughout. Frequent reference to pupils 'hovering sympathetically' near the caretaker in the scenario printed here emphasise this understated reaction, but there is no doubt about the pupils' real commitment to solving the plot. On the day I observed this programme, I was secretly trailed all through the town by a group of pupils during the lunch break, as they were anxious to make sure that I was not involved in the plot on any level, and did not want to miss any clues I might be about to let slip.

In *Factory*, the pupils are invited to view the conflict subjectively from the point of view of either the shop floor or the office/managerial department, and much of the early part of the programme is devoted to building up identification with one side as opposed to the other. It is only by this sense of loyalty being aroused that the pupils will be willing to enter into the arguments which dominate the afternoon session about the acceptability of the new scheme devised by management to the workers on the shop floor. The two sets of pupils are given totally different experiences, even down to the glass coffee cups and saucers served out in the panelled hall to the office staff, as opposed to the battered tea mugs dished up in the ill-ventilated cubbyhole to the cutters, markers, rufflers and pressers. There is a wilful polarising of attitudes, so that when the two sides meet, they have difficulty communicating and are shocked by each others' selfishness and apparent obtuseness. One side is exclusively concerned with profitability and the viability of the firm, and the other is obsessed with working conditions, the need for consultation and a living wage. This division is essential if the ensuing search for a compromise solution is to be a faithful representation of the real thing, with all its difficulties, social barriers and differing political perspectives. Because of the physical environment which effectively emphasises the differences, and because of the actors' ability to insinuate base motives to the opposing side while building up understanding, conviction and loyalty within his own, the simulation can feel far more real to the pupils than would be possible in some of the simulation games they may have played in school. Simulation, the development of an accurate but fictitious parallel to reality, is a valuable way of seeing round a problem. The fundamental issues are isolated and the key concepts illustrated. The addition of actors in roles portraying different attitudes enormously increases the verisimilitude and emotional impact of such confrontations and is far more likely to have a lasting effect on the participants as a result. As Robert Witkin says in his influential book on the arts in education *The Intelligence of Feeling* (Heinemann 1974) 'Using symbols is simply a more mobile, flexible and efficient way of organising experience and thereby making sense of the world and of one's being in the world.' (page 9.)

Workshops

The workshop which follows a play is of course quite a different form of involvement, and although it may necessitate more activity and movement, it is in fact a rather more cerebral affair. There are occasions where the workshop is a particularly appropriate accompaniment to a programme and *Snap Out Of It,* an earlier publication in the Methuen Young Drama series by Leeds Playhouse T.I.E. company, is a case in point. After they have been carefully distanced and protected from the painful subject of mental illness by the black humour of the play, the pupils are exposed by the simple but powerful techniques of the workshop to some sense of the isolation suffered by the victims of mental illness. The pupils who play out the various games in the practical session which follows *Example* are aware that they are being asked to explore consciously the themes of the play. Again their practical involvement and the tasks they are asked to perform are at a level well within their competence, but they are asked to see the connections between them, and to link them to the play in a manner which will tax them intellectually. They are being asked to generalise out the experience they have received from the particular events explored in the play, and to see that it can be related to their own lives and experience through the archetypal situations they are given in the workshop.

Many companies now view this technique with some reserve, and feel that it is somewhat superficial compared with other forms of participation more intrinsic to the particular programme, and certainly the Coventry team do not use this kind of workshop any more. Other companies who have produced *Example,* such as the Bolton Octagon T.I.E. company and the Cockpit T.I.E. team, have preferred to use the 'hot-seating' method, whereby the pupils have an opportunity to question the characters from the play, still in their roles, and to make suggestions to them which might cause them to review their attitudes and behaviour, or at least attempt to justify themselves. This technique is particularly effective in secondary shows where the play ends on a question and there is still the possibility of taking action. *Sweetie Pie* was a case in point, and in the Cockpit team's production, the 'hot-seating' technique was used to great effect, the pupils' probing questions and advice going a long way towards resolving the characters' difficulties. In these circumstances, the pupils feel that there is a definite point in questioning and advising the characters who may well act on their advice, whereas in *Example,* the events being historical and their conclusion known, the pupils' interest and advice are of necessity academic.

There is a growing trend nowadays to put the workshop prior to the performance so that the pupils respond first to direct experience, and this makes a richer background for their vicarious experience in the play which follows. This has the obvious advantage of not running the risk of hammering the play to death by immediately demanding that the pupils bury their emotional involvement and see it as a set of issues.

Readers may think that the workshop sounds like the sort of activity which the classroom teacher would arrange when the company has left the school, but at secondary level one can never be sure that such follow-up initiatives will be taken. Each teacher sees the class concerned far less of the time than is the case in infant and junior schools, and there are other pressures on teachers' time which come between the desire to pursue the T.I.E. programme and the practicality of doing so. Because there is great pressure on the pupils too, companies often have difficulty finding bookings for their secondary work unless it ties in closely with exam texts. Further, teachers who want a class to take part in a whole-day show are aware that large numbers of their colleagues, not to mention the school computer, are going to be disrupted, and there is understandable reluctance to take on the whole system in order to book a programme which is an unknown quantity.

Where teams have been established over a long period and have built up a good relationship with local schools, these problems are not insuperable, but still secondary shows are notoriously the slowest to book. Teams have had to go out of their way to make contact with the different departments in secondary schools to whom their cross-curricular programmes might be relevant, such as careers, humanities, history, community studies, social studies, as well as the more obvious English and drama departments, since all these seem to exist as so many water-tight compartments. The latest idea, pioneered by the Greenwich Young People's Theatre, is to offer 'blanket coverage' of a particular year group by spending a whole week in one school and offering a special showing of the programme to all staff who might be prepared to pursue it in their classwork. On certain key issues like race relations or unemployment, this makes very good sense, and causes fruitful ripple effects in the staffroom to boot, but one cannot always throw such a wide net over departments, and then the company are at the mercy of one or two teachers in each school as far as bookings and follow-up are concerned.

For this reason one finds that teams who have been ten years in a particular town have never been inside certain secondary schools, and one wonders whether in these schools the staff have any idea what sort of educational experience their pupils are being denied. Perhaps the publication of these scripts will go some way towards opening doors for T.I.E. teams and allowing their fresh approach to matters of curriculum to permeate a few musty corridors.

NO PASARAN

Devised by the original cast

Written by David Holman

Introduction

I think for the people in our company, primarily born in the 1940s, this is not just a subject, but *the* subject. More than any other it is something which is part of our lives and we would want to pass on some understanding of it to our audience – children born in the 1960s. It is disturbing for us to realise that in Germany, France, the occupied Low Countries and in the UK, the 'Final Solution' has become almost a secret subject again. The emergence of far right political parties has accompanied this growing ignorance.

In Bolton, and Manchester, the areas where we intended performing the programme, there are sizeable non-white populations and Lancashire is a significant area of recruitment for racist parties. It is for this reason that *No Pasaran* concentrates on the racialism and 'scapegoatism' within European Fascist ideology.

The period covered by *No Pasaran* fell within all the History Syllabuses we knew about and this, for a Company which has had a continued difficulty in attracting upper secondary audiences, was an important consideration. We knew that the programme could be justified to both 'academic' and 'non-academic' classes. It is of course unfortunate that only syllabus subjects will attract the teachers of 'O' and 'A' level subjects but that is a fact we have to deal with.

In this programme none of the major figures of European Fascism appear – there is no Hitler, no Franco, no Mosley, no Mussolini. In choosing this subject area we were sure that we should show the rise of Fascism, not in the Reichstag or Berchtesgarten, but in a school, a gym, or on a street corner. A five person company can, I suppose, do a Nuremburg Rally or a Reichstag debate, but it can do other things much better. The choice of sport as the secondary subject within the programme was made because, as a Company which is very interested in sports of all kinds, we found that the position of Jewish sportsmen under the Third Reich illuminated and explained many of the concepts we wished to put over. The fact that within weeks of Hitler coming to power every German football team, boxing club, tennis club, etc., was forced to drop Jewish players was for us a startling one, and we hope that it is communicated in the show. Interlinked with the boxing story we follow the same process in the German schools and here too, we felt this was much more immediate for our audiences than an attempt to analyse in detail the high level political developments.

Neither Cable Street nor the Nuremburg Trials are seen through the eyes of the principal protagonists and the same rationale is true of these events. In every scene in the play, bar one, either Jan Goldberg or Sammy McEvoy are present; this gives us a continuity through character which was essential to any success the programme has. This show has no discussion period following it for quite obvious reasons. The ending is very low key and emotional and we had no wish to force a quick reaction from the audience.

Working Method

The group started with documented material on the Battle of Cable Street (supplied by BBC-2's *Yesterday's Witness* which had done an excellent half-hour programme on the subject.) A natural progression backwards into Germany in the early thirties followed from that and we decided the programme had to end with an understanding of the extermination camps. This demanded a strong central character and the boxer Jan Goldberg emerged.

The Company, having had considerable devising problems over the last two years, allowed sufficient time for both this and the writing of the script. There was a devising period of four weeks followed by 2½ weeks for the full script, during which time four of the Company rehearsed parts of the script as they became available. Perhaps 75% of the script proved totally workable and on the remaining 25% a very fruitful reworking was done at great speed. Once the play was fully rehearsed no changes were made in performance.

David Holman

First performed at Bolton Theatre Studio – January 1977

Original Cast:

MIKE KAY	Jan Goldberg
DAVE SWAPP	Manfred Muller; Hamburg Nazi Party Member; Sammy McEvoy
SUE JOHNSTON	Frau Schmidt; Frau Gruner; Waitress; BUF Leader; Mrs. Riley; Miss Bronowski
SIMON MOLLOY	Kremers; Hitler Youth Leader; Nazi Education Ministry Official; Herr Schmidt; Nazi Olympic Games Organiser; Phil the boxer; BUF Member; Dr Faulkner; Tram Driver; Gestapo Officer; Nuremburg Records Clerk
DAVE HOLMAN	Wolfgang; Nordwig; Boxing Coach; Munich Olympics Delegate; Waiter; BUF Member; Hospital Orderly; Scottish Communist; Albert Riley; Nuremburg Lawyer.

First half

Audience is seated on the three sides of the acting area and enclosed
within a structure of gymnasium wall bars. A screen for the
projection of captions and photographs is set at the end, which forms
a square with the three-sided audience. Blackout. Tape: Sound of
boxers training. Slide: Germany, Summer 1932. Continue sound of
boxers training. Slide: While the German Olympic team competes in
Los Angeles the young Jewish boxer trains for the 1936 Games. Lights
come up on JAN GOLDBERG and MANFRED MULLER, two
sixteen-year-old schoolboys. MULLER holds a sparring cushion which
GOLDBERG has to try to hit cleanly as MULLER dances away from
him. MULLER is acting as coach and encouraging his friend to work
harder. He shouts punch combinations. Tape: Sound of BERLIN
RADIO NEWS THEME as MULLER and GOLDBERG continue to
spar.

NEWS: As Germany prepares for yet another National Election the
    big question is whether Adolf Hitler's . . .

    (Slide: Hitler with Brownshirts.)

    . . : National Socialist Party will make even more staggering gains
    this time. In just four years the Nazi Party has increased its vote
    from a few hundred thousand to over thirteen million votes.

GOLDBERG: Skip the politics. How are we getting on at the Olympics?

NEWS: Street battles continue here in Berlin . . .

    (Slide: Brownshirts street battle against Communists.)

    . . . as the Nazi Party's private army, the S.A., go on the rampage.
    Their targets are as usual, the Communists, who have also made big
    gains in recent elections, and the Jews.

GOLDBERG: What have we done this time?

MULLER: Double left!!

NEWS: Unemployment.

    (Slide: German unemployed. Boxers change to working with
    medicine ball.)

    Figures published today show six million Germans now out of work.
    Disturbingly more than twenty per cent of Germany's manual
    workers are now on the dole. Unemployment will again be a big
    factor in the coming elections.

    (Slide: Five Olympic rings.)

    And now for the news from Los Angeles.

GOLDBERG: About time!

NEWS: Following the failure of our National athletics team to win even a single Gold Medal, comes news that our boxers have done equally badly. However, the venue for the next Olympics has been finalised and we are pleased to announce that the 1936 Games will be held here – in Berlin.

(Tape: Radio theme.)

BOTH BOYS: Hurrah!

GOLDBERG: And I'll be there. You wait. I'll be there. The Berlin Basher, Jan Goldberg, in four years time. The night of the Olympic Finals – welter-weight division.

MULLER: You'll be middle or light heavy by then, Jan. You're still growing.

GOLDBERG: Yes, I will won't I? The crowd goes silent here at the Olympic Stadium. All eyes are on Goldberg, the German Eagle on his vest.

MULLER: Excuse me . . .

GOLDBERG: The tension mounts.

MULLER: Excuse me, but there are one or two little things to be done before you fight in the Olympics.

GOLDBERG: All right. All right.

MULLER: Hardly worth mentioning. Very trivial. Just the German Schools' Championship this weekend.

GOLDBERG: Thank you.

MULLER: Then the German Youth Championship next year, the Senior Championship in two years time when you're 18. Nothing to bother about.

GOLDBERG: I said all right!!

MULLER: Right then, get everything else out of your mind but next Saturday night. And its not the Olympic Stadium but a grubby little sports hall in Hanover. In that corner Manfred Sieloff from Dresden; great right hand according to the coach, at least three pounds weight advantage according to the coach, fit as a flea but with one little weakness . . . (MULLER points to his jaw. GOLDBERG playfully hits it. Tape: Sound of smashing glass and 'Jews Out' chant. GOLDBERG goes up to window. Young Jewish schoolboy enters.) What's going on out there?

KREMERS: It's a gang of Brownshirts. They're smashing up all the Jewish shops in the street. They've thrown Mr Lippmann through his own window.

GOLDBERG (to MULLER): You'd better get out the back.

MULLER: What for?

GOLDBERG: Because in a couple of minutes time there'll be some bricks coming through these windows. You think they're going to leave it alone? There's a sign outside with 'Hertha Jewish Lads Boxing Club' on it. Go on; get home, it's not your fight.

KREMERS: Go on, Muller. They're only after Jews.

MULLER: Oh, didn't you know? Look. (Bends his nose down.) See that? Now remember what the Coach says — a good straight left will deal with anything.

(Take up boxing positions. GOLDBERG throws KREMERS a chair to use. Fade down lights. Tape: Chants up in volume. **Blackout.** Tape: Windows broken. Slide: Through the summer of 1932 attacks on Jewish businesses and houses increase as Germany's government lurches from crisis to crisis. Tape: Sound of school bell with sound of children. MULLER on with classmate.)

MULLER: And then in the third round he just got a quick chance at a wide open jaw and . . . (woof).

(NORDWIG on.)

NORDWIG: Quiet, he's coming.

MULLER: My Lords, Ladies and Gentlemen, undefeated and after last night's contest at the Hanover Sports Hall, the new schoolboy Champion of Germany, your classmate, Jan Goldberg, the Berlin Basher.

(GOLDBERG has come on. He has the German Eagle on his track suit top. It is admired, but MULLER has brought out his new acquisition — a fart cushion.)

MULLER: My fellow pupils, behold — a new and fantastic invention from the U.S.A., delight your friends for hours, it says here. Quiet, and I will demonstrate. (Blows it up. Sits down on it -- big fart and laughter). Brilliant.

NORDWIG: Quick, teacher's coming.

MULLER: Nobody split to Mrs Schmidt. (Puts cushion on teacher's chair with another cushion over it). Then she won't know who did it.

(MRS SCHMIDT on.)

MRS SCHMIDT: Good morning Form 5.

ALL (mumbles): Morning Mrs Schmidt.

MRS SCHMIDT: I said 'Good Morning', Form 5.

ALL: Good Morning, Mrs Schmidt.

(MRS SCHMIDT goes to seat. About to sit down.)

MRS SCHMIDT: Something amusing you, Nordwig?

NORDWIG: No, Miss.

(MRS SCHMIDT goes to sit down again, stops, looks at MULLER, then lifts up top cushion and takes fart cushion from underneath.)

MRS SCHMIDT: Yours, Muller?

MULLER: Mrs Schmidt, how can you make such an accusation? It could be anybody's. You have always taught us that a man is innocent until proved guilty.

GOLDBERG: Sit down.

NORDWIG: This isn't Hollywood.

(MRS SCHMIDT has placed both fart cushion and the other one on MULLER's seat. He sits down with a deafening fart.)

MRS SCHMIDT: Muller!!!

MULLER: Sorry Miss.

MRS SCHMIDT: You bought it on Saturday morning.

MULLER: Who split?

MRS SCHMIDT: No one, Muller. My husband unfortunately shares your peculiar sense of humour. He was behind you in the queue at Schulz's Joke Shop.

MULLER: Here, not that man with the false beard! The one who bought the rubber fried egg?

MRS SCHMIDT: Yes, Muller. I had it for my breakfast this morning.

MULLER: Here, aren't they realistic Miss? When did you twig it was rubber? Did you eat it?

MRS SCHMIDT: My husband also bought something for you, Muller. (Brings out cigar.)

MULLER: Here, what a fantastic bloke. A Schulz's exploding cigar. I'll try it on my Dad tonight.

MRS SCHMIDT: No Muller. (Puts it in MULLER's mouth and lights it.) For you, Muller.

MULLER: Oh no!

MRS SCHMIDT: Now perhaps I can start my lesson. To business. Form 5 you are now starting your last year in school. At the end of this year . . . keep puffing Muller . . . you will be applying for jobs. You will know that there are six million unfortunates in Germany who cannot find work. It is my job to see that you don't join them. Puff, Muller. That means work – it means hard work. I don't mind the odd joke as long as we all work towards those examinations. Clear? Good. There is another aspect of your training which I will endeavour to help you with. Not only will you be walking out of this school as job hunters, you will be citizens as well. You will have rights and you will have responsibilities.

NORDWIG: Oh no! Not politics, Miss.

MRS SCHMIDT: Yes, Nordwig. Politics. Keep puffing, Muller. There will be elections in several weeks time and I think you should all start thinking seriously about what sort of country you want to live in. On the day of those elections we will have our own class elections. I want you all to prepare a speech and tell us the ideals you believe in. Speak to your parents, your friends, and start to clarify your ideas. Remember you are the future of Germany.

MULLER: Miss, this cigar isn't exploding Miss.

MRS SCHMIDT: No Muller. How do you feel Muller?

MULLER: Terrible, Miss. I think I am going to be sick. Can I . . . ?

MRS SCHMIDT: Dismiss, Muller.

MULLER: Aghhhhhhhhhhhh.

Blackout.

(Tape: School bell and kids getting out of school. The voice of the Hitler Youth Leader starts in the blackout.)

HITLER YOUTH: Get your Hitler Youth Paper; remember you are the leaders of tomorrow's Germany. Read Adolf Hitler's message to you.

(Lights have come up. Hitler Youth Leader in uniform has come on with papers. From opposite end comes MULLER with satchel and books followed by GOLDBERG)

HITLER YOUTH: Buy the paper of the Hitler Youth, lad. (To MULLER.)

MULLER (making to go past): Thanks I've already got that one. Come on Jan.

HITLER YOUTH: That's funny you having this one, because this is today's paper. It's only just come out. Has your friend there read it as well?

MULLER: We've got to get home.

HITLER YOUTH: No, he wouldn't have read it, would he, because this wasn't written in Hebrew, its written in German. Come on Jewboy, buy a paper. Here, this'll interest you, Jewboy, this paper. Its got your horoscope in it. It says your future's looking a bit dicey.

GOLDBERG: Is it?

HITLER YOUTH: Yea, and you know why? Have a look up the street. See those dozen big lads in brown shirts on the corner – every one of 'em is very interested in the Jewish problem.

MULLER: Problem? What problem?

HITLER YOUTH: The problem that they're still living.

(MRS SCHMIDT on.)

MRS SCHMIDT: You (To Hitler Youth.) You take your comics and peddle them elsewhere. These are school grounds.

HITLER YOUTH: This your girlfriend, Jewboy?

MRS SCHMIDT: I am the Senior Teacher at this school and I am asking you, politely, to remove yourself from the school gate so that my pupils can go home. It is quite intolerable having you hooligans outside the school every day intimidating the children. There are at least a dozen children still in their classrooms afraid to come out.

HITLER YOUTH: Oh dear!

MRS SCHMIDT: If those friends of yours aren't gone in three minutes, I am going to 'phone the authorities, is that clear?

HITLER YOUTH: You don't think the police are going to take any notice of Jew-lovers do you? Eh?

MRS SCHMIDT: Three minutes! (NORDWIG on.) Go straight home, Nordwig!

HITLER YOUTH: You're scaring me to death. (To NORDWIG.) Buy your Hitler Youth Paper and strike a blow against the Jew-lovers and Communists in the Education system. (Turning to NORDWIG.) Its disgraceful, isn't it? Communists and Jew-lovers teaching the youth of Germany now. What do you think about it, Nordwig, or or whatever your name is?

NORDWIG: Me?

HITLER YOUTH: Yes, you. Or are you another Frederick the Great Secondary Jew-lover like your teacher there?

NORDWIG: No.

HITLER YOUTH: Its over-run with Israelites, this school. Like having rats under your floorboards. Still, we know what to do about rats under the floorboards, don't we? Here, you're not a Jew are you?

NORDWIG: No.

HITLER YOUTH: You sure?

NORDWIG: No. Yes.

HITLER YOUTH: Yes, you're a Jew?

NORDWIG: No I'm not.

HITLER YOUTH: You've got very curly hair.

NORDWIG: So have lots of people.

HITLET YOUTH: Lots of Jews.

NORDWIG: I'm German,

HITLER YOUTH: Let's see your nose. Uhuh. Em. All right, then Nordwig, as a German, what are we going to do about all this?

NORDWIG:All what?

HITLER YOUTH: All these Jews at your school. What do you think of these Jews, Nordwig?

NORDWIG: I'm not interested in politics.

HITLER YOUTH: They're dragging Germany into the slime, Nordwig.
I think its about time you did your duty.

NORDWIG: I'm still at school.

HITLER YOUTH: Of course I'm assuming that because you tell me
you're a pure-blooded German, that you love your country.
Maybe I'm wrong.

NORDWIG: I do.

HITLER YOUTH: Maybe you couldn't give a shit about whether
Germany is weak or strong.

NORDWIG: Course I do.

HITLER YOUTH: Maybe when you look at an old soldier like me who's
been through the Great War for youngsters like you, and has come
back defeated because the Jews and Communists have sabotaged the
war effort, maybe you have a good laugh.

NORDWIG: No I don't.

HITLER YOUTH: I'll tell you this — every Jew in this country is a
saboteur. They're under orders from the Jews who run Russia to
keep this country weak. Did you know that?

NORDWIG: No. That's not what we get taught in school.

HITLER YOUTH: Of course you don't, because you've got Communist
teachers. Why have we got six million unemployed? Who's got their
jobs?

NORDWIG: I don't know. The Jews?

HITLER YOUTH: The Jews. But you still couldn't give a shit. I'll tell
you what, Nordwig, you're going to walk out of this school straight
on to the dole queue and I care about that, the Hitler Youth cares
about that, Adolf Hitler cares about that. So what do we do about it?

NORDWIG: I don't know. I'd have to know more. I'm still at school.

HITLER YOUTH: See my comrades up the road.

NORDWIG: Yes.

HITLER YOUTH: Four of them are still at school.

NORDWIG: How are they there when we come out if they're at school?

HITLER YOUTH: They don't like school. They have more fun selling
papers, having discussions with these Jews down here. Now you look
at them, Nordwig, and then look at yourself. See the difference.

NORDWIG: Well, they're smart.

HITLER YOUTH: Yes, they're smart. They're proud of their appearance;
in uniform, proud of Germany's military traditions. They're not
lounging round street corners, they've got an aim in life — to make
Germany the greatest country in the world. Sixteen, seventeen years

old, physically fit, they'd walk through fire for Adolf Hitler. That's the sort of movement you'd be getting into.

NORDWIG: I'll think about it. I'm interested but I've got to go. I've got things to do.

HITLER YOUTH: You've got nothing to do. Have you? What things? We've got a Hitler Youth branch two streets away. We're having a dance tonight with one of the girls' branches and tomorrow we go to the pool.

NORDWIG: You've got your own pool?

HITLER YOUTH: This party has got every facility for youth. We're built on youth. Sunday we're taking a coach into the mountains. There's nothing too good for the youth who join us. All day Sunday we'll be in the mountains. Food laid on. Our own coach to take you there.

NORDWIG: I couldn't afford that.

HITLER YOUTH: Free. Absolutely free. Come on, I'll take you round. Meet the boys. See what you think. Make sure you get a place at the pool tomorrow.

NORDWIG: All right, but I haven't said I'd join.

HITLER YOUTH: Of course you haven't. By the way. That Yid, Goldberg, where does he live? **(Blackout.)**

(Slide: In spite of the growing Nazi strength in Parliament the S.A. grow impatient to put their policies into action on a national scale. GOLDBERG, shadow boxing.)

MRS GOLDBERG (off): Jan, come and have your dinner.

GOLDBERG: A minute, Ma. Its the last round of my world title fight . . . (to himself) blood from a deep gash in his forehead streaming into his eyes: can he hold on for a points decision? Suddenly, he sees that the World Champion is dropping his guard, he's as done in as I am. Right. (Aims big punch.)

(Tape: Breaking glass. **Blackout.** Chant: 'The Yids, the Yids, we've got to get rid of the yids.'

MRS GOLDBERG (off): Jan — stay in your bedroom.

GOLDBERG: I'm coming down.

MRS GOLDBERG (off): Stay there! Stay there!

(MULLER on. Lights up.)

MULLER: What did they do?

GOLDBERG: Well, when I finally got down it was all over. You should have seen the place. Every window broken. In big letters on the door they'd painted up 'Jews Live Here'.

MULLER: Israel Goldberg's grocery store? Who else is going to live here — Hindus?

GOLDBERG: Glass in the apples. Good tomatoes ruined. What have they got against us? We're one percent of the population according to my Dad. Outside they're chanting 'Jews get out' and 'Germany for the Germans'. I was born here. My father was born here. He's got a German passport. He goes to his strongbox, gets out his passport and goes to the door. They're still heaving bricks and shouting. My Dad — I was proud of him, steps out into the street dodging the stones, holding out his passport to the man in front. 'Gentlemen,' he says, 'Gentlemen,' I ask you, Muller, you should have seen them. 'Gentlemen,' he says, 'there must be some mistake. My papers, Gentlemen. It says here — Israel Goldberg, German Citizen.' He read it out to them. They're dumbfounded. They have never seen such an idiot. Twenty of them, armed to the teeth, and there's the old man slowly reading out every little sentence in his German passport. 'There,' he says at the end, 'that makes me a citizen of Germany, Gentlemen. The Republic says so, it is signed.'

MULLER: What did they say to that?

GOLDBERG: Nothing. Well, for a minute they said nothing. He's there holding up his passport like it was the tablets of Moses. Then one from the back says, 'You Jew Bastard, for the moment you're a citizen of this rotten Republic, but remember this, it hasn't got long to go. Then you and all your tribe are going to be citizens six feet under the ground.'

MULLER: Bloody hell! (Blackout.)

(NORDWIG on. Nazi flag held by another S.A. officer. Does oath.)

S.A.: Repeat after me. In the presence of this blood banner which represents our Fuhrer.

NORDWIG: Repeat.

S.A.: I swear to devote all my energies and my strength —

NORDWIG: Repeat.

S.A.: — to the saviour of our country — Adolf Hitler.

NORDWIG: Repeat.

S.A.: I am willing and ready to give my life for him.

NORDWIG: Repeat.

S.A.: So help me, God.

NORDWIG: Repeat.

S.A.: Wolfgang Nordwig, you are now a member of the Hitler Youth — Heil Hitler!

NORDWIG: Heil Hitler! (Blackout.)

(Tape: School bell and kids. Slide: While elections take place in Germany Form 5 hold their own class elections. NORDWIG and GOLDBERG sitting among audience.)

NORDWIG: Fellow pupils of Frederick the Great Secondary School,
Mrs Schmidt wants to know what we want for our country. Well I
know what we don't want. We don't want rats under our floorboards.
A few weeks ago I went to my first political meeting, a rally at
the public park and Adolf Hitler was coming to speak. Now I wasn't
a Hitler Youth when I went to that meeting, far from it. I'd been on
a couple of trips to the mountains with them and that was great,
but I didn't want to know about any meetings. Anyway they kept
on at me and I went, just for a laugh really and I didn't have anything
else to do. There were 60,000 people in that stadium to listen to
him — 60,000. You know that feeling when you're at a big match,
the Germany v Austria game or something like that. You're standing
there at ten to three, waiting for the teams — then you see a
movement down the tunnel, red shirts, it's the Austrians. Boo, go
home, we're going to stick six past you. Then you see our boys in
their white shirts coming up from the tunnel and everybody goes
mad, shouting 'Germany! Germany!' singing the National Anthem,
and you feel like you're ten feet tall. Well, when Adolf Hitler came
out it was like that. Then it all went quiet and he started to speak.
I'd gone along for a laugh like I said, but you know, he was speaking
every word personally to me. It was up to the Youth of Germany,
me, to put Germany back where it belongs, on top of the world.
That's where the German race belongs because we're the superior
race. Its amazing because we don't get that taught in school, but
it's true. He explained it. Well what stands in our way? Its the Jews
and the Communists, and us German youth have to be in the front
line against these aliens in our midst. Hitler said would we help him
to root them out. You could have heard that crowd ten miles away.
60,000 people telling him we would. Well all of those people will be
voting today and they'll be voting Nazi, and millions more besides.
This time we're going to win. From the six of us in this class who've
already joined the Hitler Youth, there's a message — alright, you
haven't got a vote in today's election, but you can help us serve
National Socialism in this school, by rooting out all the aliens here,
not only among the pupils, but among the teachers. No more rats
under the floorboards. Heil Hitler!

GOLDBERG: The Nazi Party has done our friend Nordwig a great
favour — him, and thousands like him. They've told him what to
think and what not to think. Who he should like and who he
shouldn't like. More than that though, they've told him that he's
something special. He's the new Germany. The new German
Superman. Me, they've told me the opposite. Me, the Jew, or the
Negro, the Slave, or the Gypsy. We're scum, we're vermin; they're
putting down the rat-traps for us. I think that the German people
will have realised what the Nazi Party is about. Its against the
workers, but they lie about that. Its against the Unions, and they
lie about that. All of what they say is crap. There was a Nazi meeting
on our street last night. They come into the Jewish areas regularly
now. This example of Nazi intelligence that was speaking told his

audience that every important development in the entire history
of man was the product of a German. 'All the rest,' he said, 'was
rubbish.' Naturally I was standing well clear, but near me listening
was this little old man. 'All the product of a German,' he shouts out.
'That's right, Grandad.' Well then he started. 'Here, what about
Plato, he was a Greek, Gallileo, an Italian. Shakespeare, English.
Spinoza – a Jew.' That did it. They probably thought all the others
were footballers, but when he mentioned a Jew, three of them came
over. He was still shouting when three of these new German supermen
started putting the boot in, calling him a Communist, calling him a
bastard, calling him a Jew. The Nazi Party has done something for
Nordwig and its done something for me. I'm a Jew. Before the Nazis
came along that didn't make me any different from anybody else in
this school. They were friends of mine who used to call round for
me at the shop. Remember that Karl? Do you remember that Dieter?
I give you the National Socialist Party, the party of fear, the party
of cowards – your party, unless you stop it.

NORDWIG (over last two lines): Jewish lies!! Jewish filth!! Heil Hitler!
Heil Hitler! Heil Hitler!

(Tape: Drum beat. Blackout. Slide: In January 1933 Adolf Hitler is
made Chancellor of all Germany.

Slide: The Nazis call a national boycott on all Jewish shops, businesses
and newspapers.

Slide: S.A. on guard outside Jewish shop. Sign says 'Buy German Goods'.

(MRS SCHMIDT on with exercise books and shopping bags. Husband
appears with new joke nose and moustache.)

SCHMIDT: What do you think?

MRS SCHMIDT: Darling, I've had a very hard day. I'm tired and I've got
books to mark.

SCHMIDT: Of course. I sympathise. What do you think?

MRS SCHMIDT: Very funny.

SCHMIDT: Hours of fun it says. I shall wear it to work tomorrow. Now
what have we got to eat? I'm starving. Nothing in the larder. Well, I
say nothing. There's a mouse in there with a tin opener in its paw –
waiting. What's here? I could eat a horse. Not a horse, is it?

MRS SCHMIDT: Take it. Go and cook something while I mark the books.

SCHMIDT: Now what shall I find here; a culinary spectacular I have no
doubt. (Takes something.) Ah, yes! A feast. (Takes something else out
in a printed paper bag.) What's this???? (Whispers.) What's this?

MRS SCHMIDT: Ehr

SCHMIDT (whispering): What's this?

MRS SCHMIDT: Why are you whispering? (He gestures.) What do you
mean? (Repeats his gesture.)

SCHMIDT: Next door — they listen.

MRS SCHMIDT: Let them listen.

SCHMIDT: What's this?

MRS SCHMIDT: Pickled herring.

SCHMIDT: I can see it is pickled herring.

MRS SCHMIDT: Then why are you asking?

SCHMIDT: This.

MRS SCHMIDT: A paper bag.

SCHMIDT: From?

MRS SCHMIDT: Rosenblum's Delicatessen.

SCHMIDT: Exactly.

MRS SCHMIDT: Well — go and cook something.

SCHMIDT: Rosenblum's a Jewish shop.

MRS SCHMIDT: Thank you, I know.

SCHMIDT: Good Lord, the National Socialists have called on every German citizen to boycott Jewish shops.

MRS SCHMIDT: Yes. I know.

SCHMIDT: And you haven't. Awkward as usual. I've got a good job. And I don't want to lose it.

MRS SCHMIDT: And I've got a few principles. I don't want to lose them. Mr Rosenblum is our local grocer. He's cheap as grocers go. He's on the corner. He's open at the times I can shop, and he's very polite.

SCHMIDT: Agreed. Exactly. Come in lads, shoot me if you want to but we won't change grocers. My wife thinks she's Joan of Arc.

MRS SCHMIDT: Oh very funny.

SCHMIDT: I was in the city centre today. I wasn't going to take any notice of the boycott either, but there were uniformed Nazis outside every Jewish shop. I went to Finkelsteins, the bookshop. This Brownshirt stopped me. 'You want to buy German goods, don't you? Well this is a Yid shop.' I stood back, thinking about it. A woman brushed past me. The Brownshirt said the same thing to her. Well, she said something rather rude and went in anyway.

MRS SCHMIDT: Good for her.

SCHMIDT: Exactly. My thoughts exactly. I was about to go in myself, but then this Brownshirt called up a Party photographer from round the corner and when the woman came out — SNAP. Get it?

MRS SCHMIDT: Get what?

SCHMIDT: She's on the files. She's got some trouble coming to her. You don't want that sort of trouble do you?

MRS SCHMIDT: No.

SCHMIDT: Well then.

MRS SCHMIDT: What book were you going to buy?

SCHMIDT: Conjuring for beginners by Eames and Elvy.

MRS SCHMIDT: I'll get it tomorrow.

SCHMIDT: Not from Finkelsteins, you won't.

MRS SCHMIDT: I will.

SCHMIDT: Why can't you mind your own business?

MRS SCHMIDT: It is my business.

SCHMIDT: Listen, listen. They know how you vote, you know.

MRS SCHMIDT: Who do?

SCHMIDT: The Nazis. I had it today from a man at work. He told me how it was done.

MRS SCHMIDT: Nonsense. It's a secret ballot.

SCHMIDT: A Party member stands outside the polling station and makes a list of the order everyone goes in. He gets the names later from another one inside. Now each voting slip is numbered. All they have to do is to check the numbers when the notes are counted and they know exactly which way you voted. There's a Nazi Party member in this chap's block of flats. Came up and congratulated him on the way he voted. Day after the last election. They've got it all on file. Everything. Your photo coming out of the Rosenblum's Bookshop could be in the developing tray right now. Once you're on file, that's it.

MRS SCHMIDT: Yes, but what is it?

SCHMIDT: I don't know, but it is not worth taking the risk, is it? Be sensible. I mean, don't get me wrong — some of my best friends are Jews, but . . . **Blackout.**

(Drum beats.) Caption: Lawyers, judges, doctors, chemists and civil servants of Jewish descent — *Forcibly Retired*. Caption: First concentration camps set up by the S.A. for 'political undesirables'. Caption: Boycotts and terror against Jews increase. Caption: In the first three months 37,000 Jews flee Germany. Through this the sound of MULLER and GOLDBERG sparring. Lights up on them. MULLER is flaked out.)

MULLER: I'm taking your advice. I'm giving up smoking definitely.

GOLDBERG: Come on. I've got a fight Saturday. I've got to get in shape. (Continue boxing. Club boxing coach on.)

MULLER: Coach, save me. He's killing me here. What's he going to do to Kapellman on Saturday is nobody's business.

GOLDBERG (Ali as Frazier): Oi'll moider him, Coach. Plaster 'm all ova da ring.

Jan in training for the schoolboy championships.

COACH (holding open letter): Jan, have you got a minute?

MULLER: What is it Coach? That's a Federation envelope, isn't it?

COACH: It's about Jan. Its personal.

MULLER: Oh yea. Nobody ever writes to me. I just carry the bucket and sponge. Jan!

COACH (as GOLDBERG continues to hit sparring cushion): JAN!

GOLDBERG: Yes, Coach, What is it? (GOLDBERG comes and sits and takes off gloves. Coach hesitant.)

COACH: Em . . . Jan. It's this letter.

GOLDBERG: What is it, Coach? Do they want me to fight somewhere?

COACH: No Jan, its not that: it's . . . (Looks up and sees MULLER.) Hold on a minute, Jan. (Goes over to MULLER.) Muller help me out please. (Coach hands MULLER letter. MULLER reads.)

GOLDBERG: What is it?

COACH (while MULLER finishes reading): Just a minute, Jan.

(MULLER finishes letter and realises that the COACH wants him to tell GOLDBERG the contents.)

MULLER: Come off it, Coach.

COACH: Please.

(COACH goes slowly leaving MULLER with the letter. MULLER holds it out to GOLDBERG who doesn't take it.)

MULLER: O.K. Let's get it over with. From the German Amateur Boxing Federation to all Affiliated Clubs. For immediate implementation. Registrations of all boxers, coaches and referees of Jewish descent are cancelled forthwith. No facilities of any kind are to be offered to such people. Any German participating in a contest in which a Jewish fighter or referee takes part will be banned for life. This instruction is in line with similar actions being taken by all other German Sporting Federations.

(As GOLDBERG reads letter – Slide: German sports team including male and female athletes.)

RECORDED VOICE: Rudi Ball, Germany's foremost ice hockey player. Jewish. Banned. (Drum beat. Slide: Another athlete scarred out.)

RECORDED VOICE: Dr Daniel Prenn. Germany's No. 1 Lawn Tennis Player. Jewish. Banned. (Drum beat. Slide: Another athlete scarred out.)

RECORDED VOICE: Helene Mayer. Olympic Gold Medallist, Fencing. Jewish. Banned. (Drum beat. Slide: Cross off female athlete. Slide out.)

GOLDBERG (reading from letter): All Jewish boxers will be automatically stripped of any titles they may hold.

(GOLDBERG takes off International vest.)

RECORDED VOICE: In Wurtembourg the Jewish Organiser of a Sports Centre which he has spent his life building up, is banned. He commits suicide. (Drum beat. Blackout.)

(Caption: National Socialist Education Ministry. Lights. Nazi official behind the table. Nazi flag on table. Mrs Schmidt on.)

NAZI: Heil Hitler! (He waits after saluting. She doesn't.) I see. Now Mrs Schmidt. Senior Teacher . . .

MRS SCHMIDT: Frederick the Great Secondary.

NAZI: I understand from your note that you wish to make a complaint.

MRS SCHMIDT: I most certainly do. The two Jewish teachers on my staff have been dismissed by your Department. No reason given.

NAZI: No, Mrs Schmidt, that is incorrect. All Jewish teachers within the city have been instructed to take an immediate leave of absence. That's all.

MRS SCHMIDT: Without pay?

NAZI: Of course.

MRS SCHMIDT: Then they've been sacked. There's no difference, none whatsoever. This matter will be taken up by the Teachers' Union.

NAZI: The Teachers' Union has been dissolved. Under National Socialism Trade Unions are . . . superfluous. Nothing else, is there?

MRS SCHMIDT (pause): Yes. There is. This sheet has been distributed around my staffroom by our most junior teacher, a Mr Schildkraut.

NAZI: Yes. We know his work.

MRS SCHMIDT: He is telling my staff that not only will the school curriculum be changed to include a new subject — Racial Science — whatever that is, but that it will be taught from this sheet. Listen to this garbage. This can't have the approval of your Department surely? We are to instruct the children that 1, the Jewish Race is inferior to the Negro Race; 2, that all Jews may be recognised by their crooked legs, fat bellies, hooked noses and untrustworthy looks; 3, that Jews are responsible for having started the Great War. My God! my husband's two best friends were killed in Flanders — both Jews.

NAZI: Don't digress, Mrs Schmidt. Thank you.

MRS SCHMIDT: 4, they are to blame for the peace treaty, for the great inflation, for the present unemployment; 5, all Jews are communists; and 6, the Jews rule Russia . . .

NAZI: . . . and they do, Mrs Schmidt. The list you've just read out seems to me a reasonable beginning for the sort of instruction in racial science we wish to have taught in the schools. Yes, we would certainly authorise that.

MRS SCHMIDT: Do I understand that I must teach this . . . gibberish that your Mr Schildkraut has drawn out of the recesses of his diseased imagination?

NAZI: No, Mrs Schmidt — you will not be teaching racial science. I recognise that your ideas are very hostile to National Socialism. It is not our wish that young German minds be in your charge. Not for the moment anyway. I am instructing you to take an extended leave of absence. You must clearly be given time to re-assess your views.

MRS SCHMIDT: You mean change my mind. Teach that nonsense.

NAZI: No. Re-assess your rather, if I may say so, communistic views. You are clearly under the influence of Jewish idealogy. For the moment, Mr Schildkraut will take your place as senior teacher.

MRS SCHMIDT: Schildkraut? He's totally unqualified. (MRS SCHMIDT starts to leave.)

NAZI: On the contrary, Mrs Schmidt. On the contrary. Before you go, Mrs Schmidt — how many children in your class?

MRS SCHMIDT: Thirty-eight.

NAZI: How many desks?

MRS SCHMIDT: thirty-five.

NAZI: Overcrowded.

MRS SCHMIDT: Well, build some more schools.

NAZI: No need. (Takes paper.) Three of your class are foreigners. They can be expelled.

MRS SCHMIDT: Foreigners? There are no foreigners in my class.

NAZI: Three. Abraham Solitski.

MRS SCHMIDT: German.

NAZI: Jewish. J. Isaacs.

MRS SCHMIDT: German, he's German.

NAZI: And J. Goldberg. Heil Hitler! (Her dismissal.)

MRS SCHMIDT: Where will they go?

NAZI: Heil Hitler.

MRS SCHMIDT: WHERE WILL THEY GO?! (Blackout.)

(Drum beats. Caption: It is three years later. Slide: Olympic Games Berlin poster 1936. German band music to Nazi Party Members on from Hamburg and Munich.

MUNICH: I couldn't believe my eyes. Jews competing for Germany again after all the work we've put in.

HAMBURG: Our members in Hamburg are very upset.

MUNICH: I'm sure they are, my friend. What do you think the Munich people feel when they open their party newspaper and find Yids selected for the German team? National Socialism started in Munich. They're tearing their hair out some of them.

HAMBURG: I've been asked to protest very strongly.

MUNICH: Protest? I've got letters of resignation from Party members who have been with us since 1923. My 'phone didn't stop yesterday. Just because we host an Olympics – I never thought we'd have to throw all our principles overboard just to hold an Olympics.

HAMBURG: I agree, and Berlin – knee deep in American niggers – its disgusting.

(Nazi official on.)

OFFICIAL: Heil Hitler!

BOTH: Heil Hitler!

OFFICIAL: From Munich, I believe (shakes hands) and Hamburg (shakes hands.) The Fuhrer has asked me to welcome your delegation to Berlin, and to thank you for putting yourselves at the disposal of the Olympics Committee. I couldn't help overhearing your comments and let me say straightaway, the Party sympathises with your feelings.

MUNICH: I should hope so, Sir. The Nazi Party is going to the dogs if I may say so.

OFFICIAL: Gentlemen, Adolf Hitler attaches the greatest possible importance to the success of the Olympic Games. The greatest possible importance. There is a great deal of hostility from certain countries to our policies; our anti-Jewish programme; the imprisoning of Trade Unionist communists, priests and other scum. Germany is not yet strong enough to ignore this hostility. We are not interested in these Olympics for reasons of sporting ideals – 'it is not important to win but to compete' — all that rubbish. We are using them to show that National Socialism is disciplined, is well organised, is efficient and to impress foreigners that National Socialism is here to stay and they'd better get used to it.

MUNICH: That is understandable, but why must we have Jews in the German teams?

OFFICIAL: Don't speak as if there is a flood of Jews. Two Jews — two. The American Jewish community wanted to stop this Olympic Games and we have taken the sting out of their campaign by selecting two Jews. The Fuhrer demands this small sacrifice.

MUNICH: But look at these letters of resignation. Can I assure my people that our anti-Jewish policy has not changed?

OFFICIAL: Absolutely. You have that from the Fuhrer personally. Absolutely no change, and tell them this — the number of Jews that have left the country since we came to power has now passed the 100,000 mark.

HAMBURG: 100,000?

OFFICIAL: Does that sound like we're ditching our Jewish policy?

HAMBURG: No.

OFFICIAL: Does it?

MUNICH: No. No. My members will be very pleased to hear . . . but look, I've got a hundred party members from Munich here, and we've been assigned to the American team. We have to deal with niggers now. What do I do when I meet a nigger?

OFFICIAL: You act politely. You shake hands. You smile — yes smile. You act as if you were shaking hands with a human. Offend the U.S.A. and you will be in serious trouble. Is that clear to both of you?

HAMBURG: Quite clear.

MUNICH: Yes.

OFFICIAL: There are international considerations that the Fuhrer must take account of as he plans Germany's future — your role is not to question but to obey. (To HAMBURG.) Your members will take charge of our German national team and you have an important job to do with them. Its incomprehensible to me, but some of our own athletes seem to think that all these niggers and Yid athletes from abroad are their comrades, as long as they're good high jumpers or discus throwers they'll put their arms round them, have their photographs taken together — a disgusting example for our youth. The German team has one task, to prove that the German race is superior, mentally and physically to all other races. In brief, they must grind those American niggers into the track. They were slaves — they still are slaves, and if they win medals . . . well, they won't, will they? I hold you personally responsible. One last thing, a month ago we ordered local branches to remove all anti-Jewish signs from shops, roadsides and houses in your areas; a week ago a Belgian Olympic official travelling from his capital to ours reported his disgust at seeing such signs in every town he passed through. The Fuhrer was very angry. We've done a check. (Caption: It is dangerous for Jews to enter this town.) Fifteen such signs still up in Kassel. (Caption: Sharp bend. Slow down. Jews 100 k.p.h.) This sign still up in Garmisch. (Caption: No medicines allowed to Jews.) This sign, one of at least twenty still up in Munich. (Looks at Munich party man.) Munich!! (Caption: No food served to Jews.) These still plastered all over the city centre of Hamburg. You have until tomorrow morning.

MUNICH: I'll get on the 'phone to my party headquarters immediately.

HAMBURG: Immediately.

MUNICH: Of course — we'll destroy them.

OFFICIAL: No need, no need. Put them to one side — they can be replaced as soon as our foreign visitors have left the country. Heil Hitler!

BOTH: Heil Hitler! (All off. **Blackout.**)

(Caption: Goldberg out of work for most of the previous three years, as companies refuse to hire Jewish labour, finds himself outside his old boxing club. There are two signs up, one which says *Hertha, Berlin Boxing Club,* and below that one which says *Positively No Jews Admitted.* The CARETAKER is taking this one down. There is one waiting to be put up which says *Training Headquarters British Olympic Team.*

GOLDBERG: Hallo, Mr Gruner.

GRUNER: Its not! It is! Jan Goldberg, the Berlin Basher! Don't time . . . cor . . . last time I saw you . . . cor look at you now . . . what is it — middle — light heavy?

GOLDBERG: Middle. Just.

GRUNER: You must be . . . what?

GOLDBERG: Nineteen.

GRUNER: Course you are. Must be. Been Boxing? Course you haven't. Excuse me for asking. Here, these boys in here these days, Jan, wouldn't have lived with you — you'd be back in your dressing gown what . . . thirty seconds I'd give 'em. Punch? Couldn't punch their way out of wet paper bags, some of 'em. (Looks at sign which he still holds.) Disgrace to the country, this is. I'd break it over my knee. I would. Wouldn't do any good though. Caretakers — two a penny.

GOLDBERG: Here, does that mean I can get in? I'd give anything to have a go on that big bag — still there?

GRUNER: Jan, if it was up to me you could live in the place. You know what I think of these Nazis. Don't spread it around but you do know,

don't you? It don't mean I can let you in. (Points to British sign.)
Ask them, they're in charge from today.

GOLDBERG: When do they get here?

GRUNER: This afternoon.

GOLDBERG: Right, I will.

GRUNNER: No look, I was only joking. I'll get it in the neck. Come
back here. I've said nothing to you, right? I haven't seen you.

(SAMMY the English boxer on. Union Jack on jacket or jersey. Two
pairs of gloves over his shoulder.)

SAM: Friedrichstraaas. Hindenberg Platz? Why can't they use proper
words. I'll never find it! Here, I'll never forget that day — the first
time I met Jan Goldberg. We'd had the opening ceremony and by the
way, what a circus that turned out to be. I thought I was in a military
parade — must have been ten soldiers for every athlete. (Pictures:
Opening ceremony with soldiers.)

I thought the Olympic Games was supposed to represent peace — not
according to the Nazis. There were some near me. Lapel badges with
S.A., S.S. I didn't know what those meant at the time. They had
skull and cross bones on their hats — and that was pretty apt from
what Jan told us later. Anyway, forget that carnival — next day I
went down to the gym we'd had loaned to us to train up for my first
fight. Well, I say I goes down there, trust me, I get lost, don't I?
(GOLDBERG on with Olympic programme.)

Lucky for me I see this kid. Trouble is I don't speak a word of his
language. (To GOLDBERG.) Excusez . . . moi . . . oh no, wrong
lingo . . . em me. (Points to badge.) This is hopeless. Hertha Boxing
Club. Is near? Oh my Godfathers!

GOLDBERG: Good morning. Lovely weather for the time of year we
are having.

SAM: I'm in luck. He speaks English.

GOLDBERG: One lump of sugar or two.

SAM: Almost.

GOLDBERG: English. Oh yes. The play Hamlet from Wilhelm
Shakespeare. To be or not to be.

SAM: Very good. Hertha Boxing Club?

GOLDBERG: Hertta.

SAM: Well, whatever you call it I'm looking for it.

GOLDBERG: I know (indicates programme) you are Mr Sammy McEvoy.
Middleweight Champion, British Isles. You fight Harold Borg the . . .

SAM: Norwegian.

GOLDBERG: . . . Norwegian on 7th August in the first round.

SAM: Ten out of ten. Hertha Gym?

GOLDBERG: Its just here. (SAM starts to leave.) Please! You want that we should (boxing gesture).

SAM: Want − a sparring partner? Joking − we haven't got money for sparring partners.

GOLDBERG: My services are entirely free.

SAM: Look 'ere . . . what's your name?

GOLDBERG: Goldberg. Jan Goldberg.

SAM: Look, Jan − that's very hospitable of you, old kiddy, but look, I'm an international boxer. When I hit people I hurt 'em.

GOLDBERG: That's OK, you won't hurt me. Please?

SAM: Well, look. All right. It'll get me warmed up. What are you?

GOLDBERG: Middle-weight, like you.

SAM: You're on. Inside.

(GRUNER on as they go off. GOLDBERG winking at MR GRUNER.)

GRUNER: No, no Jan − you can't go in there − no Jews. They'll have my guts for garters. You want the Gestapo round? Want me put in a camp? All right, all right. I didn't see nothing. I wasn't here. I was sweeping up round the back − I didn't see 'em come in. (Off as lights fade.)

(Lights up on GOLDBERG and SAMMY coming in putting gloves on. Following spaces through minute of boxing.)

SAM: If I hurt you − sing out.

GOLDBERG: If I hurt you − you sing out, too. (Hits him.)

SAM: Cheeky herbert!

(Fight on. Very evenly matched. Another U.K. boxer enters called PHIL. He watches fight with interest.)

PHIL: Here Sam, this boy you found on the street?

SAM: Yea.

PHIL: Well, I should put him back there, Sam, he's showing you up.

SAM: I haven't started yet.

PHIL: Oh, my mistake. (Pause while he watches.) German, is he?

GOLDBERG: Yes.

PHIL: Here, Sam, if he isn't good enough to fight for Germany you'd better not run into the one who is.

GOLDBERG: I am good enough.

PHIL: Well, why aren't you fighting then, big head?

GOLDBERG: Because I'm a Jew. Just a bloody Jew.

(GOLDBERG starts really smashing into SAM – we must see it as the years of frustration coming out and being taken out on SAM. The other two recognise it, too, as PHIL jumps in to stop it. SAM grabs GOLDBERG.)

SAM: Look, what's the matter with you? This is supposed to be sparring. Don't you know nothing? I've got a fight in three days time and I don't want my face pushed in.

GOLDBERG: I'm sorry. I haven't had a fight for three years.

(GOLDBERG runs off throwing off gloves.)

SAM (pause): Phil, be a good 'un. Run after him. Fetch him back. (PHIL goes.) That upset me. A good little fighter like that, not allowed to box. Still, Phil managed to catch him and he was round every day after that and he didn't half give me a good work out before the Borg fight, which I might point out I won. Even took us round to his parents – a little shop, boarded up – handsome people an all – his old Dad. 'Gentlemen,' he said Phil came with me – 'you bring great honour to my house' – a boarded up shop; makes you sick. But, as I say, Jan, he was a good little pro – he didn't say anything more about this Jewish business, till Phil and me had both got eliminated. He knew it would take our minds off what we were in Berlin to do. And, of course, what he was going to tell us wasn't just interesting information – both of us, Phil in Manchester, me in East London, we'd had the old Fascist top twenty round our streets already. The Yids, the Yids, we've got to get rid of the Yids. (GOLDBERG on.)

SAM (shouts): Phil come here. (PHIL on.) Here. (To JAN) – tell him what you've just told me.

GOLDBERG: All right; Phil, in England, did you ever hear of Dachau?

PHIL: No.

GOLDBERG: Ravensbruck?

PHIL: No.

GOLDBERG: Sachsenhausen?

PHIL: No. Why, what are they?

GOLDBERG: They are concentration camps. The S.A. and S.S. have set up camps outside our biggest cities. Sachsenhausen is only a few miles from here.

SAM: There you are. Set up by the S.S., right, those mugs that were herding us round at the opening ceremony. The ones with the deaths head up here.

PHIL: But what are they for? I've never heard of them.

SAM: Neither had I, see. That's what he's saying. We just don't know what's going on over here.

GOLDBERG: They are used to imprison people, to torture and to murder any one in this country who stands up to Hitler.

PHIL: Without trial, you mean?

GOLDBERG: Yes, without trial. The S.S. and the Gestapo – they make the laws to suit themselves.

PHIL (silent whistle).

SAM: Handsome, isn't it? Here we've got to get this spread around back home, Phil eh? There's been rumours but the working people haven't got a clue about this what Jan's been talking about.

PHIL: Yes you're right. Who's coming for a beer?

GOLDBERG: I'll tell you what I'd like to do. It's the track finals tonight, and I'd like to see Hitler's face when his German Supermen come up against the American negroes.

SAM: That's a smashing idea, Jan, but the tickets went weeks ago. Look – next best thing. All those cafés on the main street where you can sit outside – they've all got wirelesses. We'll go down there and have a beer at the same time. What do you say?

GOLDBERG: Great.

(All three go off. Tape: Café music. Two waiters out, one sets tables.)

1ST WAITER: Come on, Fritz, get some work done.

2ND WAITER (FRITZ): I shouldn't be working at all. We're not going to get any customers in here tonight – there's nobody about. Everybody will be at the track and that's where I would have been if I could have got a ticket.

1ST WAITER: I'd like to be there, too. I'd like to see those niggers ground into the track.

2ND WAITER (FRITZ): They're great.

1ST WAITER: They're scum.

2ND WAITER (FRITZ): They might be, but they're going to win.

1ST WAITER: Eh? We'd never live that down. Is it on the wireless?

2ND WAITER (FRITZ): Any minute now. (Look for customers and then go.)

GOLDBERG: Hey Phil, you see that Chemist over there, Manheims. Until last week there was a notice there 'No medicines served to Jews'. The same at the grocery next door – you see the patch where the notice was.

PHIL: Its unbelieveable, this.

GOLDBERG: And next week when you've all gone they'll be up again, I bet. Now, do you want to try this café. I've been kicked out of here three or four times. Now I'm with you, of course, they won't dare.

SAM: Here, Jan, do us a favour – go and sit over there.

GOLDBERG: But why?

SAM: 'Cause I'd like to see this for myself.

GOLDBERG: Right (They sit at separate tables and WAITER comes out with tray and cloth.)

WAITER: Yes sirs, what can I do for our English guests? Beer?

SAM: That gentleman over there was before us.

WAITER: Ah, of course. (WAITER quickly sees who is at the other table but has to continue to smile back at the other table as he deals with GOLDBERG.)

WAITER: Good evening, sir. (Sotto voice.) Get lost.

GOLDBERG: Pardon.

WAITER: We don't serve kikes here. We don't like rats near our finely polished glasses, get it. Now, get lost.

GOLDBERG: That's very nice of you. A beer, please.

WAITER: Get lost. (Then coming back to the others.) So sorry, sirs, I think he's lost, looking for another place.

PHIL: I thought I heard him ask for a beer.

WAITER: Now what can I get you my dear guests? We National Socialists, Adolf Hitler himself, has a great liking for the English – we are the same people.

PHIL: Hear that, Sam? What an honour – we're the same as the great Adolf.

SAM: I feel warm inside – three beers.

WAITER: Of course – three beers – you are only two.

SAM: We're expecting somebody.

PHIL: Turn up the wireless, please, its time for the first race.

WAITER: Of course. (He goes. JAN is signalled over. Slide: Olympic Crowd. WAITER brings over the three beers. Narked to see GOLDBERG with them but puts them down as radio starts.)

RADIO: And now for the first event of the evening in the Olympic Stadium, the race which will decide who is the world's fastest human – the 100 metres sprint. The eight finalists are waiting in a line behind their blocks as they wait for the starter's instructions. Above them Chancellor Hitler is sitting with his guests. (Slide: Hitler at Olympic Stadium.)

The Chancellor is studying the line of runners and will no doubt have high hopes of the German sprint star Dietmar Zeenk in lane two. Zeenk's main opposition is in lanes 7 and 8 where the two Americans . . . (Slide: Metcalf and Owens)

Metcalfe, the Olympic Silver Medallist in Los Angeles and the new negro sensation Jesse Owens, are now getting into the blocks.

WAITER: GERMANY, GERMANY, GERMANY.

BRITISH: OWENS, OWEN, OWENS.

RADIO: A hush goes over this crowd of 100,000 people — the starter's gun is raised. (Slide: Owens at marks.)

Get set. (Bang.) They're away, cleanly and . . . this is extraordinary for a sprint race. Owens is already in a three yard lead. Metcalfe is second and the rest nowhere. Metcalf. Metcalfe is closing on Owens but he isn't going to make it. Owens. Owens wins now, by a clear yard. (British cheers. German WAITER slumps.) Metcalfe second, Osterdarp, Holland third. The time is 10.3 equalling the world record and setting a new Olympic record. (Slides through this of Owens in flight. At the end slide of Hitler very angry. WAITER clips FRITZ one who has been enjoying the race.)

FRITZ (going): The long jump will be on soon. Jesse Owens is in that too.

PHIL: Jan, what I said earlier about what you're going to do. What I meant was, you're a good boxer, come to England, you'd get fights as a pro, wouldn't he, Sam?

SAM: Indubitably.

PHIL: Yea.

SAM: We've got a spare mattress — put it on the floor in the front room. Be pleased to have you, and there's lots of Jewish people in East London. You wouldn't be short of a bit of company.

GOLDBERG: What about my parents?

SAM: Look, come over, earn some dough, lots of venues in the East End, then send for them when you're fixed up. Think about it. Waiter!

WAITER: Yes, sir.

GOLDBERG: Three more beers, please.

SAM: How's the master race going on down at the stadium then tosh?

WAITER: Very well, sir, thank you. We are about to win the long jump.

SAM: Oh?

WAITER: Yes, sir, the German champion, Lutz Long is leading by a mile — last jump to go — Owens is nowhere.

PHIL: Let's hear it then.

(WAITER turns the radio on. Goes to get drinks. Slide: Lutz Long.

RADIO: Long of Germany leads with 7.87. I can see the Reichchancellor above us, a broad smile on his face, as he looks down on the blonde figure of the German champion. (Slide: Hitler Happy.)

The café owner boasts about Germany's superiority.

Owens, who has been jumping very badly tonight, is on the runway
for his last jump — he is said not to like this event and never to train
for it. He does, however, hold the world record — he is on the run up
for his last jump. Long has already jumped and Owens has 7.87 to
beat. (Slide: Owens.)

Into his run now, a smooth rythmical powerful action, approaches
the take off board, stamps down and (cheers) an enormous jump.
The result — we're waiting for it. 7.87 to beat. Owen's jump is
8 metres and 7 centimetres. Owens wins again. (Slide: Hitler mad.
WAITER stalks off.)

GOLDBERG: A toast. Jesse Owens — according to Adolf Hitler a
sub-human.

BRITISH: Jesse Owens.

GOLDBERG: And one more. To Jan Goldberg in England.

PHIL: Good boy! (Hugs him.)

SAM: I'll drink to that.

PHIL: You'd drink to anything, you would!

SAM: Yea. (Toasts.)

GOLDBERG: Sam, lend me a pencil and some paper — I must write a
note to my parents.

SAM: There you are. We'll get out of your way. (Go and sit at another table.)

GOLDBERG: Dear Ma and Pa, my new friends have invited me to England with them. (GOLDBERG continues to write as commentary begins. Start of 200 metre race commentary as they get ready to leave the cafe.)

RADIO: And now here in the Olympic Stadium, the last event of the night. The runners are in their blocks for the final of the 200 metres for men. All eyes on the inside lanes where the crouching Americans wait for the gun. Lane two Robinson and in the inside lane the sensational negro Jesse Owens. The starter raises his gun (bang). A clean start but Owens, it looks like Owens must be tired after his previous efforts, he's not away at all well, and Robinson has the lead. Through the first bend and its Robinson in lane two from Owens in lane one. Through the second bend and it's still the two Americans. These two black figures almost together as they stride into the straight and sensationally Owens is clawing back that lead. He's attacking his compatriot and the lead is gone. It's gone. Owens breaks the tape . . . now. The time . . . this is sensational — the time a new world record 20.7. Owens looks up at the Chancellor's box but Adolf Hitler has gone. The Fuhrer has not been here to witness this great negro athlete win his third individual gold medal. Listen to the crowd. OWENS, OWENS, OWENS, etc.

(WAITRESS enters and indicates that GOLDBERG should leave.)

GOLDBERG: A hundred thousand of them cheering a black man. Tomorrow when they go to work they'll see signs of all over Berlin again — 'No Jews welcome here'. Negroes, Jews, to you National Socialists we're just animals. But tonight of one of us animals is the toast of Berlin. That's funny.

(Tape: OWENS! OWENS! OWENS! Chant then fade. Blackout. House lights.)

Second half

Slide: Union Jack. Tape: Land of Hope and Glory, as audience returns.

Slide: An East End Street with *London's East End 1936* superimposed on it. Enter three Blackshirts who go to the three sections of the audience. All make different short speeches, along these lines:

BLACKSHIRTS: We're down here in the East End today to tell you the policies of the British Union of Fascists, policies for a free British people. Britain for the British. Not Britain for the Wogs, not Britain for the Jews, but Britain for the British. You just listen (Main B.U.F. speaker on platform.)

1ST BLACKSHIRT: Fellow Britons, I'm glad to see such a big crowd down here today, but then we always get a big crowd down here in the East End, don't we? Why? I'll tell you for why. One, because the British Union of Fascists and National Socialists is the only party which speaks the truth to you. (Slide: Blackshirts photo.)

Two, because our Leader, Oswald Mosley . . . (Slide: Photo Oswald Mosley) is the only man in this country who has the will to lead Britain back to greatness like what Mr Adolf Hitler has done in Germany. (Slide: Blackshirts March.)

The British Nazis have got the answers to the questions you're asking in the East End of London – why do we live in slums down here? Why ain't we got any jobs, some of us, and when we have got jobs why is the pay nuffing and the conditions diabolical? Why ain't our kids got nowhere to play? You want to know why? I'm going to tell you. You want answers. The British Nazis have answers. The East End Boroughs are the most overcrowded and slum-ridden in England. Why? Why is this? Use your eyes! Look at the shops in this street – look at the names – that'll show you why.

2ND BLACKSHIRT: Zipakalarski, Tailor; Levy & Burnstein, Furniture; Goldman's, Kosher Butcher.

3RD BLACKSHIRT (simultaneous with 2ND BLACKSHIRT): Schuman, Used Clothes; Bernstein, Grocers; Schwertzer, Carpets.

1ST BLACKSHIRT: Getting the message? Mendellsonn's, Orlovsky's, Golschmitts. Eh, Eh? Where's your Smiff? Where's your Jones? Where's your Brown? I'll tell you. They've had to scarper – they've had to get out to make room for these Yids – these Israelites . . . (GOLDBERG enters and stays behind bars) the chosen people. The people who murdered Jesus Christ on Calvary's tree. From here to the docks, they've taken over. Did you know that there's 150,000 of them in this area alone? The British Nazis are telling you that's too many – its 150,000 too many. Join us and help clear out this pestilence from your London. Not the Jews' London – your London. You Englishmen.

GOLDBERG: You say there's 150,000 too many Jews down here. I think there's three too many Nazi's down here.

1ST BLACKSHIRT: Hello, we've got the Communists out again today, shouting down free speech. Was that a little Jewish voice I heard? Was that a German Yid I heard squeaking? You see what I mean – every civilised country in the world is booting the Jews out and we're *taking them in!*

GOLDBERG: Hitlers. You're just little Hitlers. (The TWO BLACKSHIRTS have reached GOLDBERG. One grabs him round the neck and they start to work him over.)

1ST BLACKSHIRT (as GOLDBERG is beaten up): Hitler? Yes – our leader, Oswald Mosley, stands side by side with Mr Hitler. Hitler has opened our eyes – he has shown us the enemy – the stinking yid, the nigger and the alien. You saw the way he was trying to interrupt – this communist – he doesn't believe in free speech. We're holding another meeting tonight in the Whitechapel Road. Come and listen; come and join our movement; help clear the Jews out of London, out of England.

(BLACKSHIRTS exit and GOLDBERG is left on the ground. Pause. SAM enters.)

SAM: You O.K. Jan?

GOLDBERG (getting up): Yes.

SAM: They draw a big crowd in Bethnal Green these days – these Blackshirts, a very big crowd. Quite a few of you here today, aint there? And not one of you prepared to step in and stop this – eh? Not one. I helped this kiddy get out from Nazi Germany. Yes, I said, you've been expelled from school because you're a Jew; you've had your home attacked regular because you're a Jew; no one'll give you a job because you're a Jew; they've stopped you putting the gloves on because you're a Jew. Come to England, I said, we aint like that. No, I said, we've got a tradition down our way of taking in refugees and giving them a break. Well, sorry, Jan, they've made a liar out of me, this lot. Welcome to Berlin – Bethnal Green style. It's no good running away mate. Don't you see what's happening? You're disillusioned and the Blackshirts are offering you this as a sacrifice. Disillusioned? Not surprising is it. You've been through a war most of you and they told you you'd come back to live in homes fit for heroes. They must have meant those slums. You've had Tory Governments cutting your wages and then smashing your organisations during the General Strike to make sure they stayed cut. Then you've had a Labour Government helped by the TUC giving you more of the same. You've lived through the worst slump ever and it's his fault they're telling you. Couldn't happen here? Jewish kids thrown through windows last week. Couldn't happen here? A twelve year old girl hung up in White Horse Lane in a crucifixion.

Couldn't happen − it is happening.

GOLDBERG: But this doesn't make you Nazi Germany, does it? You don't have your Trade Union leaders murdered in jail; your country isn't run by the secret police; you don't live under a fascist dictatorship; you don't have concentration camps outside every city. Not yet you don't. Not yet, you don't!! **(Blackout.)**

(BLACKSHIRT enters and starts writing slogans on wall: '*England for the English*', '*Perish All Jews*'. MRS STEINER comes out and grabs BLACKSHIRT.)

MRS STEINER: Now you just rub that off. This is my house. I said, rub it off!!

BLACKSHIRT: Oh and I haven't got anything to do it with.

MRS STEINER (grabbing him): Well use your sleeve you little blackshirt oik.

(BLACKSHIRT pulls away and then throws MRS STEINER down on ground.)

BLACKSHIRT: Ger off, you old bag. Jewish filth. This your house is it? (Goes to fetch brick.)

MRS STEINER: NO!! That's my little girl in that winder!

BLACKSHIRT: Good. (He throws brick. Tape: sound of shattering glass. MRS STEINER screams.)

MRS STEINER: Sarah!!

BLACKSHIRT (kicking at MRS STEINER): We'll be back to finish you lot on October the 4th, you bag.

(He runs off. MRS STEINER calls for help. On come SAMMY and GOLDBERG. BLACKSHIRT can't escape.)

SAM: Hallo, what's going on here then.

MRS STEINER: Help me Mister.

(SAM and MRS STEINER into house.)

GOLDBERG: So you're on your own this time?

(SAM on.)

SAM: Jan, you keep hold of him. There's glass in all this little girl's face. (SAM off.)

GOLDBERG: If that little girl loses her sight . . .

BLACKSHIRT: What? You going to beat me up? Well, make the most of it Jewboy, because when we come through these streets on October the 4th I shall make a special point of finding you.

GOLDBERG: What are you talking about − October the 4th?

BLACKSHIRT: I'm talking about the biggest Blackshirt March we've ever brought into the East End. I'm talking about the day we finally show you that the yids have got no future here. Here, what you doing?

Jan takes on an East End Blackshirt.

GOLDBERG: You're coming with me to a Union meeting in the docks. You can tell them about this march – it's not us that are finished it's you.

BLACKSHIRT: You're living in a dream world, yid. You're not reading your newspapers. People are crying out for leadership and they're finding it. Hitler, Mussolini, Franco, Mosley . . . What you doing Jewboy? (GOLDBERG pushes him.) You can't win Jewboy! (Another push.) I won't forget this Jewboy. (GOLDBERG pushes him off.) **(Blackout.)**

(Caption: Bethnal Green Hospital. SAM and MRS STEINER. ORDERLY on with mug of tea and gives it to MRS STEINER.)

ORDERLY: There you are, Mrs Steiner.

SAM: How's the little girl?

ORDERLY: Mr Hayward is operating now.

SAM: What does he think?

ORDERLY: We'll just have to wait and see. (Goes off.)

SAM: He's their number one surgeon, this Mr Hayward. Your Sarah's in good hands.

MRS STEINER: This is the same thing happening here what's happening in Germany.

SAM: No, no.

MRS STEINER: No? Well, what has your Jan Goldberg been saying about what's going on in Berlin? It's exactly the same here now. You going to tell Sarah it's different?

SAM: Look, I'm not saying it's different — I'm saying that's it! That's their lot — that's their last attack on kids if I have anything to do with it.

(DR FAULKNER enters. SAM gets up.)

FAULKNER: I've just heard Sammy — what happened?

SAM: Her Sarah — a Blackshirt smashed a window in on her.

FAULKNER (to MRS STEINER, greeting): Mrs Steiner. (To SAM.) Is she all right? (SAM nods.) Sam — have you heard about a Blackshirt march into the East End?

SAM: Yes — October the 4th — we heard tonight.

FAULKNER: Well, this is what I've done. I've phoned the Mayor of Bethnal Green and he has promised to contact all the East End Mayors. Then a delegation of them will go to the Prime Minister and get it stopped.

SAM: Doc — it's a lovely idea, but them mayors won't swing it. A Tory government has never stopped the Blackshirts smashing up the East End. It takes people's minds off the two million we've still got on the dole.

(ORDERLY enters.)

ORDERLY: Dr Faulkner, Mr Hayward would like to see you.

FAULKNER: It's the Government's responsibility — this march is a blatant attack on the whole Jewish community. (Going.)

SAM: I know that — you know that — the East London Mayors know that, but the Government couldn't give a monkey's. We'll have to stop them ourselves. (To MRS STEINER.) And we will an' all.

(GOLDBERG enters with cap and package. Gives SAM a leaflet and then goes to MRS STEINER.)

GOLDBERG: Mrs Steiner, this is from the Union meeting. (Gives cap.) It's a collection towards your hospital bill, and I'm to give you this from the man in the toyshop on the High Street.

SAM: Alf.

GOLDBERG: It's for Sarah — he says you'll find out on October the 4th what East End people think about attacks on kids.

SAM (reading poster): 'All out on October the 4th — stop the Blackshirt march.' You've got your skates on tonight old kiddie.

GOLDBERG: Not me. The Trades Council are doing 100,000 leaflets on their duplicator.

SAM: Good lads.

GOLDBERG: Dockers and Stevedores pledge full support.

SAM: I should hope so.

GOLDBERG: We've had support promised from Communist Party branches, Lancashire, Yorkshire and Scotland.

SAM: What sort of support?

GOLDBERG: They're coming down – they're coming down.

(DR FAULKNER comes on with ORDERLY behind.)

FAULKNER: Mrs Steiner – Mr Hayward has completed the operation and he was able to save one eye. Sarah's still under sedation, but if you'd like to come and sit with her . . . (Indicates to follow orderly.) She's a very brave girl, Mrs Steiner. (MRS STEINER goes off with orderly.)

SAM: That's our enemy according to Mr Mosley – Jewish kids. Eight year old lads. Our enemies? When those unemployed Welsh miners marched to London they came down those Jewish streets. I remember four or five of them walking down this particular street – hungry, shabby – singing their Welsh hymns. From out of every house the old Jewish people came and they listened to what those miners were saying – how long they'd been out of work – and there wasn't a house in that street where they didn't give at least a ha'penny or a penny. So, when I'm asking people to come out on October the 4th and they say they can't be bothered or they want a lie in, or they're telling me these aint our people, this aint our fight, I'll remind them of that. **(Blackout.)**

(Percussion. Caption: Three days to go.)

VOICE (recorded): The East London Mayors have been trying to have the Blackshirt march stopped. The answer was – No.

(Caption: Two days to go. Percussion.)

VOICE: We've just heard that they're drafting in police from all over the country for this march. Yorkshire, Devon, Somerset, Lancashire. Everywhere. The Government are determined that this march will be a success.

(Caption: One day to go. Percussion.)

VOICE: The fascists have been told to assemble at 11.00 hours at the Royal Mint but we can't find out which route they're taking into the East End. We must have that route. It's impossible to close off the whole East End. It can't be done.

(Tape: crowd shouting 'All out on Sunday!' 'Stop the fascist march!' Caption: 4th October 1936. GOLDBERG enters.)

GOLDBERG: Sammy! Sammy!

SAM (coming on with scab on his face and razor): Yea.

GOLDBERG: Come on, Sammy, there's a few hundred out on the streets already.

SAM: Already? That's a good sign. (Looking.) That's a very good sign. I hope they keep turning up at this rate. (Back to shaving.) How did you get on last night? You handsome devil. (Looking in mirror.)

GOLDBERG (starting to put up banner): Oh, thank you.

SAM: Not you — me.

GOLDBERG: We did a final leaflet round the bus station, tram depot and the pubs.

SAM: Yea? What sort of response did you get?

GOLDBERG: Well, people said they'd turn up, but who knows.

SAM: Well, let's just hope it stays fine for them. Where are they sending all these people as they turn up?

GOLDBERG: They're all around the East End, Sammy — we don't know where to go.

SAM (wiping face): All round the East End — it's bleeding hopeless, Jan. If only we knew which way the fascists were going. What you got there?

GOLDBERG: I was reading in the paper last night about what's going on in Spain. It said the workers of Madrid, when the fascists tried to enter the city, put up the words 'NO PASARAN'.

SAM (looking at banner): They shall not pass — I like it; and they bloody won't. (Clears shaving kit.) Right, let's get down Leman Street, whichever way the fascists take they'll have to go down Leman Street — we'll get some barricades organised.

(SAM and GOLDBERG leaving. Enter SCOT.)

SCOT: Excuse me, Jimmy — is this the East End?

SAM: Yes.

SCOT (handing piece of paper): D'ye ken this place?

SAM: Is that your coach, mush?

SCOT: Aye.

SAM: Well, don't take it down there — there's going to be a knuckle party down there soon.

SCOT: What do you think we're down frae Glasgow fer — there's ninety of us in that coach — and it's only a fifty-six seater — know what I mean?

SAM: Welcome to London, Jock. Jan get on that coach and get them down to Leman Street — see (to SCOT) the problem is that we don't know which way the fascists are going, so if you've got a few useful boys, spread these around a bit. Jan, drop half a dozen down Leman Street, half a dozen down the Commercial Road, half a dozen down the High Street and get all the rest down to Aldgate. And see if you can get some tea organised for these boys.

SCOT: Tea (JAN taking SCOT off.) Did that man say tea — you no got anything stronger than tea?

(DR FAULKNER on in Blackshirt uniform holding map.)

FAULKNER: Hallo Sammy – have a look at this.

SAM: What's all this? (To upper window.) No, Mrs Greenbaum, he's
not a Blackshirt, dear. Look, don't throw that bottle – it's
Dr Faulkner from the Royal . . . what is this?

FAULKNER: It's a map of the route the Blackshirts will be taking.

SAM: How did you get hold of this?

FAULKNER (changing clothes): Well, I thought as I was new to London
and none of the Blackshirts would know me, I would go along and
offer my services. I got there about an hour ago.

SAM (studying map): Leman Street, yea we expected that.

FAULKNER: I just went up to the police cordon, showed them this
bag and said 'Doctor' – they allowed me through.

SAM: Commercial Road.

FAULKNER: After getting past two more lines of police I found myself
quite near to Mosley's car, where copies of that map were being
given out – so I waited and after a while I was handed one.

SAM: Bleeding hell – Aldgate?

FAULKNER: I made an excuse and came back here.

SAM: Cable Street – we hadn't reckoned on Cable Street – still, you've
saved our bacon, you have, Bob.

(Enter MRS RILEY.)

MRS RILEY: Ooo. Here I am Sammy – all ready and willing.

SAM: Mrs Riley, I'll leave this with you dear. (Pointing to end of street.)
Look, we want the end of this street barricaded because the fascists
are coming this way, ain't they?

MRS RILEY: Oh, are they? Not if I've got anything to do with it,
they're not.

SAM: That's the girl. Come on Bob. (FAULKNER and SAM exit.)

MRS RILEY (shouting at house): Albert, get up. (At another house.)
Mrs Peters. Oh, open your window, dear, I can't lipread. Mrs Peters,
listen dear, that old tin bath of yours, can you get your Tommy to
bring it up the end of the street and anything else you've got – we're
building a barricade. Albert, are you up?

ALBERT (off): Here, is that you Ma? Here, bring us a cup of tea and the
News of the World, will you – I'm having a lie-in.

MRS RILEY: You bring them into the world – for what? (Goes off.)

ALBERT (off): Mum, Mum – here, what you doing – me bed, Mum!

(MRS RILEY comes out with mattress.)

MRS RILEY: We're building a barricade, Albert – come down and
help. Now!

ALBERT (off): What about my toast?

MRS RILEY: One minute, Albert, or I'm flogging your football boots.

ALBERT (off): Coming Ma.

(SAMMY enters.)

SAM: You lads there. (To house.) We need old chairs, mattresses, boxes, the kitchen sink. That barricade needs to be bigger. I wish Mosley could see this.

GOLDBERG (starts fixing banner): I thought the idea was to keep him out.

SAM (helping with banner): No, at the end of the street there. Look at them dockers and stevedores working side by side with the Jews building barricades. The fascists try and split up Jew and Gentile and they've never been more united. How are we doing?

GOLDBERG: Aldgate's a big problem, Sam — it's just too wide a block. It's a hundred yards from corner to corner.

(Slide: trams parked in crowds.)

SAM: Here, look. Them trams ain't moving.

(TRAM DRIVER enters.)

TRAM DRIVER: Here, you're the kid who came down our depot last night asking for support to block off these streets?

GOLDBERG: Yes.

TRAM DRIVER: Well, there you are.

SAM: Great — it'll take ages to shift them.

TRAM DRIVER: Oh, no, can't be done. Without this key the engine's locked and I'm hanging on to this.

SAM: Fantastic. If we could get two more we could block the whole street.

TRAM DRIVER: Yes. We thought four and all — so Knosher Cross is bringing in the Liverpool Street tram at 11.15 — and he'll be parked over there. You've got Dennis with the 205 to Hackney at 11.26. He's going to be parking next to mine, and at noon you've got Alf's 466 to Holborn Viaduct in the space that's left.

SAM: Good boy.

TRAM DRIVER (going off): Here, you've got a good crowd out here this morning — someone told me a quarter of a million. Well I'll go and join them; if only the Hammers could get crowds like this.

SAM: That's it, Jan. (Looking at map.) Aldgate's blocked — Leman Street, Commercial Street, the High Street, Cable Street. If there's going to be any bother its going to be in Cable Street.

GOLDBERG (both going): Well, what are we waiting for?

(Slide: Cable Street. Percussion Backing. Caption: 'The Battle of

The Battle of Cable Street.

    Cable Street.' Slide: Working class crowd. Slide: Police at Royal
Mint. Slide: Mosley and police approach Gardiners Corner.
Slide: Police stopped at barricades. Slide: Running fight in
Cable Street. Slide: Workers with 'They shall not pass' written
on barricade.'

MRS RILEY: Ooo! Where is everybody — here, Mrs Peters — heard the
latest? The police have told Mosley they can't get through any of
the streets so they're calling it off — they've told him to take his
Blackshirts off up West. Here, you'd better go and get your tin
bath back dear, you know what they're like round here. Albert,
go down and get your bed. (SAMMY on.) Here Sammy, have you
heard?

SAM: I've just come back from Cable Street, ain't I? (Swing and cuddle.)
We've done it. (Start pub music.) And I'll tell you what put the old
tin lid on it — the law was in Cable Street pulling down the
barricades when all the upper windows open up and the old 'uns
the Mums with kids, start lobbing bottles, chairs, all sorts of stuff,
and the law says I'm not going through there for anybody, and
they scarpered — they didn't pass.

MRS RILEY: Well, darling, I'm off down the Dukes — they're having a
ding dong down there tonight. I'm going to have a few tonight.

SAM: Yea, well (she is going) get me one in dear. That was the biggest
knees up the East End had seen in many a long year. Pubs, caffs,

you couldn't get in. Fascism had been stopped in the East End yeah, but it was still growing in Germany, Italy, Spain — terrifying. As for Jan (starts taking down the banner) he got lots of fights — five bob a time, sometimes 7/6d — good little fighter, see. Always gave people their money's worth. And, of course, at the end of each fight he had a few more bob towards the fare which would bring over his old mum and dad to England, and by 1939 he had enough. But it was about that time that he wasn't getting any replies to his letters to them, so he decided to go back to Berlin to find them. (Drum beat.) That was the last time any of us saw him. (Blackout.) Caption: Berlin 1939.

GOLDBERG (in blackout): Ma? Pa? I've got the money.

GESTAPO 1 (in blackout): Goldberg?

GOLDBERG (in blackout): Where's the furniture?

GESTAPO 2 (in blackout): Goldberg?

GOLDBERG (in blackout): Where's everything gone?

GESTAPO 1 (in blackout): You are an enemy of the Reich, Goldberg.

GESTAPO 2 (in blackout): You have insulted the Fuhrer, Goldberg.

(Lights up on GOLDBERG standing in a spot light with a placard round his neck which reads *Jewish Spy. I am an enemy of the German people.'*

GOLDBERG: Spy! What is this?

GESTAPO 1: We've got your letters, Goldberg. (Holds them out.)

GESTAPO 2: Your Jewish scribble condemns you, Goldberg.

GOLDBERG: Where are my parents?

GESTAPO 1: Your parents are working.

GOLDBERG: I've come to take my parents away — that's what you want, isn't it? To get rid of us all. I'll take them.

GESTAPO 2: Your parents are working for the Fuhrer, Goldberg.

GOLDBERG: Where have you taken them?

GESTAPO 1: They've gone on holiday.

GESTAPO 2: A holiday camp with just some light work.

GESTAPO 1: Very light — just to keep them from getting bored.

GESTAPO 2: At the seaside — he doesn't believe us.

GESTAPO 1: Here, they've written a picture postcard to you (Hands it to GOLDBERG.)

GOLDBERG:(reading from postcard): 'WE ARE DOING WELL HERE.'

GESTAPO 2: So will you.

GOLDBERG: 'WE HAVE WORK AND WE ARE WELL TREATED.'

GESTAPO 1: Naturally.

GOLDBERG: Signed Z. Goldberg, Waldsee – where is Waldsee?

GESTAPO 2: It's a picture postcard, Goldberg.

GESTAPO 1: Use your eyes, Yid.

GESTAPO 2: They're at the seaside, Yid, because with a war threatening we want them safe, our Yids.

GESTAPO 1: We wouldn't want anything happening to the Goldbergs.

GOLDBERG: I want to see them.

GESTAPO 2: Just what we were going to suggest.

GESTAPO 1: It's a long way, though – can you afford the fare?

GESTAPO 2: (taking out JAN's wallet with money): Course he can.

GESTAPO 1: You'll travel first class with this, Goldberg.

GESTAPO 2: A one-way ticket, Goldberg, that's all that's necessary.

GESTAPO 1: Oh yes. A return would be a waste of money, and Jews don't waste money. (**Blackout.**)

(Sound of aircraft. Slide: German aircraft.)

RECORDED VOICE: In September 1939 the Polish capital of Warsaw is bombed by the German Airforce. This is the first event of total war, a war that will last six years and cost the lives of many millions.

(Tape: Dive Bombers. Slide: Dive Bombers. Tape: Bombs landing. Slide: Warsaw in ruins. Tape: Arctic wind (through next slides). Slide: Bombed buildings. Slide: German soldiers – Stalingrad. Slide: British soldiers – Western Front. Slide: American tanks. Slide: Soviet soldiers.)

RECORDED VOICE: By 1945, the German Army has been forced to retreat. As Russian, American and English soldiers liberate areas of Poland, Czeckoslovakia, and Germany – the legacy of Nazism is revealed – the concentration camps.

(Slide: Allied soldiers supervising the burial of concentration camp victims. Caption: 'Nuremburg 1946'. Slide: Nazi leaders at Nuremburg. Caption: Nazi leaders are tried for war crimes.)

SERGEANT: Excuse me, Sir – are you the lawyer in the Hess trial?

LAWYER: Yes.

SERGEANT: I've got those lists you wanted.

LAWYER: Thank you.

(As LAWYER looks at them SAM gets up and approaches the SERGEANT.)

SAM: Excuse me, Sir – I've been waiting to see someone for three days now. I was sent down here. Corporal MacEvoy, S., Royal Engineers. Did you get my letter?

million. I don't think we'll ever know. The Jews were packed in trains and delivered to various camps. On arrival there, they were given a picture postcard that they were to send to any surviving relatives. The message was printed already and it was always the same: 'Doing well, well treated'. Waldsee isn't a seaside holiday resort, I'm afraid; its a concentration camp near Munich. Its called Dachau. Your friend arrived there in June 1940. Do you want to know what happened to him? We have the death books.

SAM: Can you give me a minute?

(LAWYER comes in.)

SERGEANT: Excuse me, Mr Marsh, this is Miss Bronowski. Mr Marsh is the prosecuting counsel in the case against Rudolph Hess.

LAWYER: Thank you.

(SERGEANT goes back to desk.)

SAM: Yes. Could I see the books, please?

SERGEANT: Just take a seat, old chap – I'll see to it. (SERGEANT goes.)

LAWYER: Miss Bronowski, over the next weeks, we will be putting on trial the surviving officers and guards of the Auschwitz concentration camp. Today we are beginning the trial of the Camp Commandant, Rudolph Hess, and as one of the few survivors of that camp we will need your evidence. In court, I shall have to ask you several questions which will no doubt be very distressing for you. I deeply regret having to ask you things which will evoke memories. I'm sure you would sooner forget, but you understand the reason.

MISS BRONOWSKI: Will Hess be there? In the court room? (He nods and she breaks down. SERGEANT gets coffee out and LAWYER takes it over.)

LAWYER: He can't hurt you anymore, Miss Bronowski. Now, may I go over with you the questions I shall have to ask in court. (She nods.) I'll first of all, ask your nationality.

MISS BRONOWSKI (very quietly): Polish.

LAWYER: And at what age were you brought to Auschwitz?

MISS BRONOWSKI (very quietly): Fourteen.

LAWYER: I'm sorry, Miss Bronowski, but I shall have to ask you to speak louder than that in the courtroom. Now at what age were you brought to Auschwitz?

MISS BRONOWSKI (slightly louder): Fourteen.

LAWYER: Good. Thank you. And when did you first see the man Rudolph Hess? Start at the beginning.

MISS BRONOWSKI: We had been brought in a train, thousands of Jews, from the Warsaw ghetto, all with our yellow stars. They were cattle wagons. In Warsaw, the guards forced us into the wagons, eighty, a hundred to each one, I couldn't tell. I don't know how long the journey took, without water. We were covered with our own filth — nobody could move, many died. The stronger men killed, just to get somewhere to sit — do you understand?

LAWYER: Yes.

MISS BRONOWSKI: The doors were finally opened and it was like being released from hell. We didn't realise then that across the railway sidings was a greater hell; the camp of Auschwitz. We were kicked and beaten out of the wagons by S.S. guards. The man Hoess was giving the orders. Two lines were made; the old people and the very young in one line, and the young and strong ones in another line.

LAWYER: These lines were made for what reason?

MISS BRONOWSKI: The one line was taken straight to the gas chambers. The others to work.

LAWYER: Were these people told they were going to be gassed?

MISS BRONOWSKI: No. Hess announced that everyone was going to take a shower and since we knew that this was a regular practice in Polish prisons, many believed it. A little way from these bath houses there was an orchestra playing. Jewish girls, young girls, all in white, playing 'The Merry Widow'.

LAWYER: Go on.

MISS BRONOWSKI: They always played very loudly and they never played a slow tune, always quick ones. Of course, there was a reason. The bath houses were not bath houses at all, but gas chambers, and the orchestra played to drown the screams of the dying. I was lucky, you see. I had a gold medal for the violin. I became part of that orchestra.

LAWYER: Now, I believe you have information on a certain conversation involving Rudolph Hess later that year.

MISS BRONOWSKI: Yes — he often came to listen to the orchestra, and on this occasion he had arrived back at the camp after being away for several days. The orchestra was silent at this moment because the gas chambers were being emptied.

LAWYER: Of . . .

MISS BRONOWSKI: Yes. Hess was saying to another officer that he had just come from visiting Treblinka, another extermination camp in my country, where the camp commandant had told him that 80,000 Jews had been liquidated — that was the word they always used — in the course of half a year. Hess had learnt that the method used was poisoning with carbon monoxide but that he could do better, it was very inefficient, and that he had ordered new equipment which would improve the Treblinka record.

LAWYER: And what was that equipment?

MISS BRONOWSKI: A new building was built, and in the death chamber a new chemical was used. It was known as Zyklon B. It was much quicker than before. You could tell this immediately in the orchestra because before we had to play for perhaps twenty-five minutes of music from the first to the last of the screams, now only ten minutes or twelve.

LAWYER: Can you tell me how many people were gassed at one time?

MISS BRONOWSKI: I understand two thousand. Hess was heard to boast about this new record. At Treblinka at that time only two hundred could be killed at one time.

LAWYER: Was Hess present when people were sent to the bath houses?

MISS BRONOWSKI: Quite often.

LAWYER: Could you tell me about the new process which Hoess had installed?

MISS BRONOWSKI: You must remember that in a camp there are very few guards. It is always possible that when people know they are going to die then there will be trouble for the guards. In Auschwitz they overcame this by deceiving people as to what was happening to them. The gas chambers themselves were not sinister looking places. They were underground, and above them was a beautiful lawn with flowers around the border. The signs at the entrance said 'BATHS'. Most people who came straight from the cattle wagons believed this, as I told you. They were told to undress because they were going to have a shower. Some were even given towels to make the pretence more convincing. Once inside the shower room a door was locked and sealed. All this we could hear. Then we would see some S.S. men walk across the lawn, because hidden in the flowers were the air vents at the top of the death chamber. A Sergeant Moll always gave the order for the Zyklon B crystals to be dropped into the vents. He would always say the same thing – 'all right, let's give them something to chew on' – that was the signal for the orchestra to begin playing because the gas was very quick.

LAWYER: One last question – were all the prisoners killed in this way?

MISS BRONOWSKI: No. For example, Hess himself had a loathing for the Russian prisoners, and many of them were killed with injections of petrol into their blood stream.

LAWYER: Thank you, Miss Bronowski. If you could just wait here – there are some other witnesses I have to see before the trial begins. Please ask if there is anything you need.

(LAWYER goes. SERGEANT brings books to SAM.)

SERGEANT: These are the death records for the Dachau camp starting from the date stamped on that postcard. Now, don't hope for too much. Bear in mind that Goldberg is a very common Jewish name. You may find hundreds, even thousands of Goldbergs in those books. You've got an initial, but that's quite common too. There are sometimes details other than names written in the end column, but you do understand that you'll probably really never know? Anyway, best of luck. (SERGEANT goes to his desk. SAM starts going through books. SERGEANT goes to MISS BRONOWSKI.)

Soon be over Miss, the lawyer was right. They can't hurt you anymore – they're finished. (SERGEANT back to desk. SERGEANT to SAM.)

They're finished. The courts will deal with Hess – that's the easy bit. But what about the next time they come out of the woodwork looking for a scapegoat, some little minority, that they can blame any new crisis on. Which is going to be next to find their names written up on walls. So and so out . . . So and so you've got our jobs, you've got our houses and we're coming after you. Hooked nose, black, brown, yellow – just so long as there's not too many of them.

SAM: Well, they'll find me waiting – and I won't be on my own.

SERGEANT: No.

(Fade lights. Slide: Goldberg in boxing pose. Tape: Goldberg's voice *'We are doing well here. We have work and we are well treated.' signed J. Goldberg, Waldsee.* **Blackout.** Slide: NO PASARAN. Houselights.)

EXAMPLE

The case of Craig and Bentley

For performance to Fifth and Sixth Formers

Devised by the Belgrade Coventry
Theatre in Education Company
Belgrade Theatre
Coventry

Introduction

The Theatre-in-Education programme *Example* had its beginnings in one of the regular 'ideas' meetings held by the Coventry team. A team member had read David Yallop's book *To Encourage the Others* and this led to a proposal that the Craig and Bentley case should form the core of one of the team's programmes. Obviously, this initial decision, taken in the course of an afternoon, was founded to a large extent on the enthusiasm of one person. Very quickly though, *Example* generated excitement and commitment from those members of the team chosen to devise the programme. After preliminary discussions and consultation with the Teachers' Advisory Panel, a number of important decisions were made about the programme. It was decided that the material was most suitable for a maximum of sixty fifth and sixth formers, and that it would be a 'whole day' schools-based programme. The first half of the day would be a performance piece, and the second, a 'workshop' session which would explore the issues further. The play was to be written by the newly appointed writer-researcher.

By the time the summer holidays began, the team had held some preliminary meetings, but the major part of their effort would take place during the four-week rehearsal period allocated after the presentation of the first draft of the script at the beginning of the Autumn term.

At the first meeting held by the team after reading the script, it was decided that it was not suitable to continue with and was put aside in its entirety. This was unfortunate for the writer, who had written his first piece for the team, largely in isolation; but he was able to accept this decision and begin work *with* the team rather than for it, a relationship which was to prove much more fruitful. The team's initial depression at the situation in which they now found themselves, was quickly forgotten when the consequences had to be faced. Three decisions were made rapidly: firstly the deadline for the first performance was extended by about a week, secondly, it was decided that the project would be group-devised, and thirdly, that it would be necessary to employ two more actors.

The actual devising period of *Example* was remarkable for the spirit it generated in the team. The injustice of Derek Bentley's execution was to prove a continual and growing spur to the team's efforts. A wide variety of devising techniques were employed in constructing the programme:- Some sections were scripted directly from improvisation; some were written by individuals and adapted, either through improvisation, suggestions from other team members or adaptation during rehearsal; and some material is taken directly from court records, books and documents. All these sources and activities were to flow together into an intense period of activity to produce the final piece. This process

Example 71

was, of course, greatly aided by the fact that the team were dealing with a definite story line, well documented in a comparatively small number of books.

It is fair to say, that the second part of the programme, the 'workshop' section was relegated, through various pressures, to a substantially secondary position in terms of the amount of time expended on it. Although the workshop changed during the run of *Example*, it never contained, for instance, any questioning of the characters in role which both the Bolton and Cockpit teams were to make use of to considerable effect in their productions. The workshop revolved around two major themes: firstly to illustrate that a great deal of the evidence presented in the case was extremely suspect, and secondly to illustrate how the various processes of the law operate against less intelligent members of society.

Finally, some notes on the intended playing of the performance part of the play. It is important to remember that *Example* is designed to affect the audience emotionally. The team devising the programme were always conscious of the enormous power of this emotion and used it to maximum effect. That is not to say wastefully or gratuitously but in the full knowledge that emotion can be used as an educational tool. For this reason Bentley was not played as a stumbling moron, but with what can only be described as dignity. While the play acknowledges and reinforces Derek's lack of intellectual capacity, it does not simply make him someone to be laughed at. It is no accident that Derek comes from the audience at the beginning of the play and his portrayal must never alienate him from the empathy of the audience. Of course, many members of the audience do laugh at him during the play, but this must never be at the expense of sympathy for his position and anger at the massive injustice which he suffered.

Harry Miller

Example

Was first presented in the Autumn Term 1975 with the following cast:

BENTLEY	Harry Miller
MRS BENTLEY/HUMPHRIES	Diana Watkins
TEACHER/CRAIG/PROCTER	Paul Swift
NARRATOR/MAGISTRATE/CASSELS/ PETITIONER/SILVERMAN	Sue Johnston
GODDARD/PARSLEY/FAIRFAX/ PASSER-BY/CROOM-JOHNSON	Robert Boyd
MILES/FOREMAN OF THE JURY/ STAGE MANAGER	John Pitt

Directed by David Young

Scripted by the Company and Stephen Wyatt

Setting

At Coventry the play was performed in traverse with a large projection screen at one end. Other settings and props were kept to a minimum.

Sources

The main material in the play is derived from *To Encourage the Others* by David A. Yallop, *The Trial of Craig and Bentley* by H. Montgomery Hyde, the biographies of Goddard by Arthur Smith and Eric Grimshaw and Glyn Jones, and *My Son's Execution* by William Bentley.

EXAMPLE

The play opens with an informal introduction by the NARRATOR, who explains that the performance is based on a real incident in the 1950s, when the children's parents were about their age. It was a period of violence, not unlike today, with people worried by the ever-increasing crime wave, the influence of American gangster films and the easy accessibility of weapons smuggled back from the war. Before the performance starts, the audience is going to be shown a newsreel in the style of the 1950s Pathe newsreels, telling them something about what was happening in Britain during the post-war years.

The NARRATOR switches off the lights and hands over to the stage manager:

Example 73

Introductory music. The newscaster's voice is on tape while the
slides are shown on the screen.

NEWS: Ladies and gentlemen, the Organisation proudly presents for
you Potted Pictorial News Magazine. Once again we bring you the
brightest and best in educational news entertainment right into the
warmth and comfort of your own school hall. Today we cover the
Post-War years.

(Loud patriotic music. Slide of V.E. Day.)

It's the 15th August, 1945, and the whole of a victorious and happy
nation is out in the streets to celebrate the ending of World War
Two. Here, enthusiastic crowds cheer and sing outside historic
Buckingham Palace, home of our dearly loved monarch, King
George VI. There's no doubt that after six years of worry and
war, everybody's really looking forward to a time of peace and
plenty.

(Slide of man trying on a demob suit.)

For our happy heroes returning home from the war — over four
million of them — there are quite a lot of shocks in store. But first
it's out of uniform and back into civvy-street clothes. And how's
this one for size, sir?

(Slide of Clem Attlee.)

General Election, 1945, and a great shock at the polls. Labour
really knocks the Conservatives for six. And so enter Clem Attlee,
head of the Labour Party and wartime Deputy Prime Minister, and
it's goodbye, at least for the present, to Winston Churchill, the
man whose speeches heartened and inspired the nation during the
war. Clem promises:

ATTLEE: A new society — free, democratic, efficient, progressive,
public-spirited.

NEWS: Brave words, Clem, but though Britain's at peace, she's still
got plenty of headaches. Housing, for instance.

(Slide of bombed ruins.)

Over half a million homes were destroyed during the War, and
there's been precious little time to build any new ones, so it looks
like an awful lot of families are going to have to go short for an
awful long time. Nor are things too hot with education.

(Slide of children boarding a train.)

It's not easy to keep schools open with bombs dropping all around
you, and so many children have not got all the schooling they
might. Many, like these children, were sent away from their
homes, and now are making their way back. All in all, it's reckoned
that it's going to take education some time to get back on its feet,
and many kids are going to have a long, hard struggle to catch up
on their reading and writing. Good luck, kids!

(Slide of a spiv selling nylons in Oxford Street.)

SPIV'S VOICE: Nylons, nylons. Genuine American nylons, lady. Only thirty-five bob.

NEWS: For housewives, nylons are just one of the many things that are still very scarce now that the war's over. Rationing still applies to most important things, and if you haven't got the coupons then you can't have the goods. Or can you? That's where spivs like this come in. Somehow or other, there's always somebody somewhere who knows how to get the things you want whether it's extra petrol or fresh farm eggs. But at a cost, of course! And when it comes to shady deeds, there are things quite a bit more serious than a little dabble in the Black Market. The first post-war crime figures show an overall increase of 50% over 1939, with more people in prison than at any time since 1912. And perhaps the biggest blow of all, there is an increase in crime of over 250% amongst young people between seventeen and twenty-one, the children who've grown up during the war years. Bad news indeed!

(Slide of Lord Chief Justice Goddard.)

And one of the men in the hot seat when it comes to crime is Rayner Goddard, who became Lord Chief Justice in 1946. Here's what he has to say about his job.

GODDARD: I have two aims as Lord Chief Justice. The first is to clear up the administrative muddle created by the war, and to make it easier and cheaper for the ordinary citizen to use the law. My second great aim is to put down the post-war crime wave which is reaching terrifying proportions.

NEWS: Well, all the luck in the world, Lord Goddard, you're certainly going to need it. Luckily, not everything's completely gloomy on the home front. Take fashion, for instance. 1947 sees the appearance of a bright new style from France — the New Look.

(Slide of woman modelling the New Look.)

Well, that should certainly make a few heads turn. But when you're buying the material, don't forget that rationing is still very much on the go, and here . . .

(Slide of Elizabeth Taylor collecting ration book.)

. . . we see lovely film star, Elizabeth Taylor and her mother, signing up for their ration books on a visit to Britain. Nobody, not even film stars, can manage without them. Have a good stay, Liz!

(Slide of a pub lit by candle.)

Winter, 1947. The coldest winter within memory. And with coal supplies unable to keep up with demand, there are power cuts in gas and electricity all over the country, and train and tram services grind to a halt. The only thing to do is gather round the piano by candlelight, keep out the cold with a drink and wait for things to get better.

(Slide of interior of hospital.)

Example   75

Luckily, there's soon to be relief for all those winter coughs and sneezes. In 1948, the Labour Government unveils the National Health Service. For the first time in British history, medical care is free to everybody, regardless of income, age or nationality. So perhaps it's not surprising that there's such a run on spectacles and false teeth in the first few weeks. And let's all look forward to a big improvement in the nation's health.

(Slide of the figure over the Old Bailey.)

Clem and his Government are not quite so lucky with another of their measures – the Criminal Justice Bill of 1948. Clem manages to stop the use of the birch and the cat o'nine tails, traditional methods of corporal punishment in Britain for centuries, but when it comes to a move to get rid of capital punishment as well, for a trial period, he finds himself hitting problems. The House of Lords throws out the abolition of hanging, lead by Lord Chief Justice Goddard.

(Slide of Goddard.)

GODDARD: I cannot believe that public opinion – or I would rather call it the public conscience – of this country would tolerate that persons who deliberately condemn others to painful, and it may be to lingering death should be allowed to live.

NEWS: Luckily, everything's still not completely gloomy on the home front.

(Slide of the Festival Hall during the Festival of Britain.)

1951 is Festival of Britain year, a pick-me-up prescribed for the nation's ills, and a reminder that Britain is still great, despite her troubles. The whole nation embarks on a spree of celebration . . .

(Slide of Winston Churchill.)

And the General Election brings the old war dog, Winston Churchill, back into power again – though many may wonder whether he'll be quite as much at home in peace as he was in war. But soon, we are to lose another great war leader. In 1952, his Majesty King George VI dies, and his young daughter, Elizabeth . . .

(Slide of Elizabeth in mourning.)

. . . returns in mourning to take over the helm of government. Almost immediately, preparations are under way for her Coronation, which will take place in 1953. Already, there is talk of a New Age dawning.

(Sound of early fifties' rock music.)

But not all aspects of the New Age will be automatically welcome to everybody. This fellow, for instance – the Teddy Boy.

(Slide of teddy boys in a cafe.)

Dressed in their distinctive uniform, the teddy boys can be seen

down the local dance halls with their girls, jiving to the latest
pop records. Doubtless, most of them are just high-spirited lads,
dressing up and having a good time, but don't forget that teenage
violence is continually on the increase, and some of these boys
seem a bit too fond of knives and knuckledusters. And talking of
crime, there's one body of men which always has to be on hand
in case of trouble — the police.

(Slide of policeman.)

Here a spokesman explains that the police have troubles of their
own . . .

SPOKESMAN: At present, the police force is desperately under
strength. The Metropolitan Force alone is 5,000 under strength
and 30% of recruits resign in their first year. Our basic rate of pay
is in fact lower than that for a dustman. And for that, we are
required to risk our lives daily. In 1951, in three months alone,
four policemen were shot dead.

NEWS: But the police are not the only people with worries about
what is happening. Other people are watching the rise in crime
and lawlessness with growing concern. Among them, Lord Goddard.

(Large slide of Goddard.)

GODDARD: I must condemn the great and disturbing increase in
crime which is disgracing this country at present, and more
especially the crimes of violence. How are we to deal with the
man who smashes a tumbler on a public house counter and jabs it
into the face of a man with whom he has quarrelled, or the man
who beats up an old man or woman in the streets? Is it not time
that our attitude towards punishment should be reconsidered?
I believe, for years past, we have thought too much of the
criminal and not enough of the victim. We cannot stand by and
watch our country undermined by growing violence and a
decreasing respect for the forces of law and order. Criminals must
be made to see that their misdeeds, particularly if they are attacks
upon police officers or others in authority, will be punished and
punished severely. Criminals will only be deterred from crime and
violence by seeing an example made. We must make that example,
now, before it is too late.

(The tape stops.)

Example 77

Scene One

The NARRATOR enters.

NARRATOR: We have come here to-day to tell you the story of that example. His name, Derek William Bentley.

(BENTLEY crosses stage and sits amongst audience. Slide of Bentley.)

Our story begins in 1947 when Derek Bentley was 14 years of age.

(Exit NARRATOR. Enter TEACHER. Blank slide.)

TEACHER: Last night, before you went home, you were all supposed to hand in an essay under the title of "Where I Live". From the work I've seen so far, I can only presume that most of you walk the streets at night. One essay — that's all I got. Johnson's. Let me read it to you. "Where I Live" by P. Johnson, 4B. "I live at 67, Nuttall Road, Croydon." Apart from three blots and a crossing out, that's it. And by the way, Johnson, there's no "u" in road. I don't have to tell you, it's not good enough. Now, I don't expect you all to be little Willy Shakespeares. I know that due to the war, most of you haven't had more than one year of school in the last five. But I do expect you to try. This is your last year and my God, I'm going to give you lot some sort of chance even if I have to put half of you in hospital to do it. Oh, and talking of hospitals, I see that we have a little stranger with us this morning. Bentley has decided to honour us with his yearly visit. Come out here, lad! Let's have a look at you. We don't get the chance very often.

(BENTLEY comes forward.)

For those people lucky enough not to remember him, this is Derek Bentley. Where have you been all this time — safari-ing in Outer Mongolia?

BENTLEY: No, Sir, I've been ill, sir.

TEACHER: Of course, silly me. And what has it been this time? Pneumonia, typhoid, leprosy?

BENTLEY: Headaches.

TEACHER: Headaches. That's very serious. I should see a specialist about that, lad. We'd hate to lose you, Bentley. I mean you're such a little ray of sunshine aren't you?

BENTLEY: Thank you, sir.

TEACHER: Who do you think you are, lad?

BENTLEY: Sir?

TEACHER: I said, who do you think you are, Bentley?

BENTLEY: I don't know, sir.

TEACHER: You don't know. Well, I'll tell you, Bentley. You are a
great useless lump of lard. You are fourteen, you are lazy, you are
stupid. Fourteen years of age, and you can't read or write at all,
can you, lad?

BENTLEY: I can a bit, sir.

TEACHER: Oh, can you, can you really? Maybe you've learned
something while you've been away. I mean, you've spent so much
time with the doctor, you ought to be a qualified nurse by now.
Alright, Bentley, if you can write, let's all see you. Here's the chalk.
There's the blackboard. Well, go on, lad.

BENTLEY: I don't know what to put.

TEACHER: Anything, Bentley. Use your imagination, lad — a novel,
a poem, a critical essay. We don't mind what you do.

BENTLEY: I can't . . .

TEACHER: Very well, then, I will help you, Bentley. Write down,
"I was ill" . . . Well go on . . . at least *try*, lad.

BENTLEY (trying): I can't.

TEACHER: No, you can't, can you, Bentley, because you're not only
stupid but bone idle as well . . . I'd like every one of you to take a
good look at him. If you want to end up as thick and useless as
Bentley, then don't bother working or trying or handing in essays,
don't bother coming to school at all. But for those of you who
want to stand any sort of chance in life, you'd better start
knuckling down to some hard work *now* — beginning with that
essay you should all have handed in yesterday. I've got to see
Mr. Hughes now, and when I come back, I'll expect to see all those
essays completed. So you'd better get on with it now.

(Exit TEACHER. BENTLEY leaves.)

Scene Two

VOICE OVER (tape): Mrs Lillian Bentley. Derek Bentley's mother.

(Slide of MRS BENTLEY. She enters very shaken and upset.
DEREK BENTLEY enters. Blank slide.)

BENTLEY: Hello, mum.

(MRS BENTLEY humphs and turns away.)

What's the matter?

MRS B: Don't you know, Derek? Don't you know?

BENTLEY: You're upset, Mum. That's all I know.

MRS B: Upset? Yes, I am upset! So would you be if you'd had the
police trampling through your house, going through your things,
and not knowing what they wanted.

Example 79

BENTLEY: Eh?

MRS B: Not knowing what they were looking for. What you'd done.

BENTLEY: What I'd done?

MRS B: Yes, Derek, what you'd done. What the hell have you been up to, bringing the police charging through the house?

BENTLEY: It's got nothing to do with me. What did they come for?

MRS B: They were looking for tools. They said you'd stolen them. What've you been up to?

BENTLEY: Nothin'. I ain't done nothin'.

MRS B: You go on that building site, don't you? The one in Sidney Street. You go there, messing about.

BENTLEY: So what?

MRS B: You were seen there. Somebody told the police.

BENTLEY: Told 'em what?

MRS B: That you took some tools from the building site – stole them, Derek.

BENTLEY: Eh? That's potty, Mum. I never took no tools. Honest I never. You know I never, don't you , Mum? . . . Mum?

MRS B: I don't know. What can I think? Police coming in your house, crashing about, looking . . . you being seen there. Derek, did you take them?

BENTLEY: No, Mum.

MRS B: Oh, Derek, you wouldn't lie to me, would you?

BENTLEY: No, Mum. Honest.

MRS B: Derek, look me in the eyes and say that. Straight in the eyes.

BENTLEY: I wouldn't, Mum.

MRS B: Alright, son. We'll . . . we'll see what we can do. We'll go to the police station. They said to send you when you came home. It'll be alright. If you didn't touch them, it'll be alright.

Scene Three

The MAGISTRATE enters at one end.

MAG: Stand forward, Derek.

> (DEREK stands in front of the MAGISTRATE. MRS
> BENTLEY stays watching.)

MAG: Derek, I've looked at your case very, very closely. I've studied the information you've given me. I've talked to your parents . . . talked to your teachers. (Sigh.)

You see, Derek, I wouldn't mind if I hadn't seen you here before.
Now, when I'm faced with the problem of boys of your age coming
back to me, time and time again, I have to say to myself, 'This
can't go on.' I've got to draw the line somewhere, haven't I,
Derek?

BENTLEY: Yes, miss.

MAG (sighs): Well, Derek, I think for your own good, I'm going to
send you away for a period of corrective training, I'm going to
send you to a place called Kingswood School. I hope, Derek,
that during your stay there, you'll take advantage of the things
it has to offer you. You can learn a lot there. Have you anything
to say, Derek?

BENTLEY: I never done nothing.

MAG: I'll be sending you to Bristol for a period of three years, Derek.
You may leave the Court now. Good luck, Derek.

BENTLEY: Three years, Mum?

MAG: Leave the Court now, please.

BENTLEY: But I never done nothing!

MAG (leaving): Leave the Court.

All leave.

Scene Four

Slide of CRAIG.

VOICE OVER: Christopher Craig, age fifteen.

(CRAIG enters miming firing a gun.)

PARSLEY (off): Hey, wait for me.

(NORMAN PARSLEY enters. Blank slide.)

PARSLEY: Hey, Chris, you'll never guess who I saw in Woollies this
morning.

CRAIG: Em . . . Adolf Hitler.

PARSLEY: No.

CRAIG: But he always buys his Spangles there on Mondays . . . No, I
give in.

PARSLEY: Derek Bentley.

CRAIG: Who?

PARSLEY: Derek Bentley . . . you must remember him . . . went to
your school — about three years above you.

CRAIG: Bentley . . . Bentley . . . Oh, wait a minute . . . Big geezer.

Example 81

PARSLEY: Yeah.

CRAIG: Thick.

PARSLEY: That's him.

CRAIG: I remember now. We used to call him King Kong.

PARSLEY: He's just left Kingswood.

CRAIG: King who?

PARSLEY: The Approved School.

CRAIG: Has he?

PARSLEY: Well, when I say he's just left, I mean he's been home six months but he's only just come out of his room. Six months. Hiding in his room. Daren't come out before, he thought people'd laugh at him. (Laughs.)

CRAIG: What's he sent down for?

PARSLEY: Nicking something or other, but he says he didn't do it.

CRAIG: Don't they all?

PARSLEY: Yeah.

CRAIG: What's he doing now?

PARSLEY: I don't know. Looking for a job, I suppose.

CRAIG: Well, I might be able to help him out there.

PARSLEY (puzzled): Eh? (Realising.) Oh, yeah! (Laughs.)

CRAIG: I'm not laughing, Norman.

PARSLEY: No . . . sorry, Chris.

CRAIG: Might be able to offer him a bit of work, help the lad out a bit. I mean he's a big lad, had experience, he could be very useful to us. I'd be interested in seeing him, Norman. Perhaps you could arrange that. Tell him I could put some work his way.

PARSLEY: But he's thick, Chris.

CRAIG: Then he'll do what he's told won't he?

PARSLEY: Yeah!

(They both laugh. PARSLEY goes. CRAIG sits and waits. Slide of GODDARD.)

VOICE OVER: It is now 1952. Lord Goddard, worried by the ever-increasing crime wave, makes his views known at a banquet given by the Lord Mayor of London.

GODDARD (tape): Nowadays the cane is never used in schools. It would have done some of these detestable young thugs good if they had had a good larruping. What they want is to have someone who would give them a thundering good beating, then perhaps they would not do it again. Instead, I suppose they were brought up to be treated like little darlings and tucked up in bed at night. Nowadays, Courts cannot deal with such boys as they should. We are faced with a widespread breakdown of discipline.

Scene Five

As the tape ends, PARSLEY re-enters with BENTLEY. Blank slide.

CRAIG: Hello, Derek.

BENTLEY: Hello.

CRAIG: I've been waiting for you.

BENTLEY: Waiting?

CRAIG: Yeah. Sit down, make yourself at home.

BENTLEY: Thanks.

CRAIG: I've been hearing about you.

BENTLEY: Yeah?

CRAIG: Yeah. People are bastards, aren't they? I mean, you make a mistake or maybe you don't do nothing at all, but they still get you, don't they?

BENTLEY: Who gets you?

CRAIG: The law, Derek, the bloody law. They put you away. Then when you get out, nobody wants to know you, do they? People laugh at you behind your back like, bastards.

BENTLEY: What are you getting at?

CRAIG: I'm just saying it must be rough for you, Derek, you know, going to an Approved School and that.

BENTLEY: How did you know about that?

CRAIG: Well, it gets around dunnit? I mean, once you've been inside, everybody knows.

BENTLEY: Yeah, looks like it, dunnit.

CRAIG: Don't worry, Derek, I mean, you're my mate.

BENTLEY: Am I?

CRAIG: Yeah, course you are. Me and Norman, we're both your mates, ain't we, Norman?

PARSLEY: Yeah, course.

CRAIG: I mean, you can trust me. I won't say nothing to no one. I'm a very trustworthy lad. Ask anybody. Ask Norman, he'll tell you.

PARSLEY: Chris is very trustworthy.

CRAIG: See, what did I tell you? In fact, I'm not only very trustworthy, but I'm very popular as well. I mean, you could say

Example 83

I had a whole *gang* of friends. Right, Norman?

PARSLEY: Right, Chris.

CRAIG: They don't like the law either, Derek, 'cos of what it does, see, to people like you. My friends they don't ever get into trouble.

PARSLEY: No, never, 'cos we've got brains, see.

CRAIG: Who's got brains?

PARSLEY: Oh, er . . . you . . . you've got brains, Chris.

CRAIG: That's right. I'm not only very trustworthy and popular, I'm also very, very clever. And I'd like you to trust me, Derek, I'd like you to be my mate.

BENTLEY: Yeah? Why?

CRAIG: Cos I like you, see, you sound like the sort of geezer I could get on with. (Snatching comic from BENTLEY's pocket.) Here, do you like comics?

BENTLEY: Yeah.

CRAIG: And gangster films and that?

BENTLEY: Yeah.

CRAIG: I love 'em. I think they're really great.

BENTLEY: Yeah, so do I.

CRAIG: See, what did I tell you? You and me, we're the same sort of person, Derek. Would you like to be my mate? . . . I mean, I suppose you must have loads of mates.

BENTLEY: I got a few.

CRAIG: How about being my mate, then?

BENTLEY: Alright.

CRAIG: My brother Niven's a gangster, you know.

BENTLEY: Yeah, that right?

CRAIG: Dead right. Payrolls mostly. He's pulled jobs all over Europe. Just come back. You should see his wallet, it's full of tenners. Big time, my brother. Mind you, we don't do so bad, do we, Norman? I mean, we have some fun eh?

PARSLEY: Yeah, Chris, we have a laugh.

CRAIG: Like last Thursday. That was a scream, that was.

PARSLEY: Yeah, laugh a minute.

CRAIG: You should have been there, Derek. You'd have enjoyed it.

BENTLEY: What happened?

CRAIG: Well, you know Jackson's, the little Post Office on the corner of Victoria Street, well we went in there, didn't we, not to buy stamps though, was it? (Laughs.) No, we went in after it was closed, like.

BENTLEY: You broke in?

CRAIG: No, I wouldn't say that. This brick in Norman's hand just bumped into one of the windows accidentally like. Anyway, we got in there. And what did we see? The till full of money, very untidy, fivers all over the place. So we . . . tidied up a bit. Doing Mrs. Jackson a favour really. Well, she must have heard us and woken up, 'cos down she trots in her little fluffy slippers and her curlers. "Who is it?", she says, "What's going on?" Stupid old slag. "Watch it," I said, "One more word out of you missus . . ."

(He produces a gun from his pocket.)

BENTLEY: Is that real?

CRAIG: . . . "And you'll be visiting your husband in heaven."

BENTLEY: Where d'you get that? Is that real?

CRAIG: Course it's real. What d'you think it is? Roy Rogers' cap gun? I'm not a kid.

BENTLEY: Has it got real bullets in it?

CRAIG: Wouldn't be much good without them, would it?

BENTLEY: You'll get put away, carrying a thing like that.

CRAIG: Not me, mate, they ain't never going to put me inside.

BENTLEY: Does he always carry that around?

PARSLEY: Yeah, all the time.

CRAIG: Don't worry, Derek. Sit down. It's safe as long as you know how to use it. My Dad taught me, and he was a marksman. He taught me and Niven. Guns aren't dangerous if you know how to use them . . . and I do. I mean, if you're professionals, you've got to be prepared, ain't you?

BENTLEY: But you wouldn't shoot anyone, would you?

CRAIG: No, 'course I wouldn't . . . not unless I had to. Don't worry, Derek, no one gets into any trouble. And you're my mate, ain't you?

BENTLEY: Yeah, yeah, 'course I am, Chris.

CRAIG: That's right. Anyway, old Mrs Jackson, she's shaking away and we hears this . . . splashing like. The old girl stood there with the gun at her head, bloody wet herself, ain't she? (Laughs.) Eh Norman, you got any money?

PARSLEY: Yeah.

CRAIG (looking at his watch): Well, we just got time to go down to the pictures ain't we? Coming, Derek?

BENTLEY: Yeah.

Example 85

CRAIG: Come on then.

(They all leave. Large slide of GODDARD.)

GODDARD (tape): It seems to me that there is a great tendency nowadays to think that the sole aim of punishment is to make people better, not to punish them for doing wrong. I have never yet understood how a criminal law can deter people from crime unless it also punishes them. The two things seem to me to follow one on the other. It is society's way of showing that if certain conduct or certain acts are persisted in, then consequences which must be unpleasant and must truly punish will result.

Scene Six

As tape finishes, CRAIG and BENTLEY come on. Blank slide.

BENTLEY: Eh, Chris, I'd better not go too far.

CRAIG: What do you mean?

BENTLEY: Well, I've got to be home soon, for me tea.

CRAIG: You're a pig, Del, that's all you think about, your bloody stomach.

BENTLEY: I can't help being hungry.

CRAIG: Neither can pigs.

(CRAIG, who has been trying doors, now finds a door or window that can be opened.)

BENTLEY: Eh, what are you doing?

CRAIG: Do you have any money?

BENTLEY: No.

CRAIG: Neither do I. I'm getting some.

BENTLEY: But somebody'll see you doing that. Look, leave it can't you?

CRAIG: Look, nobody's going to see us in this alleyway are they? Just shut up and stay with me.

BENTLEY: Come on, let's go.

CRAIG: Shut up and keep a look out will you?

BENTLEY: Look out for what? What are you doing? . . . Don't do that!

CRAIG: Look, do you want to meet the whole of Croydon Police Station all at once?

BENTLEY: No, but –

CRAIG: Well, shut up then.

BENTLEY: No, Chris, come on, leave it.

CRAIG: Look, you're supposed to be a mate of mine, ent ya?

BENTLEY: Yeah, but –

CRAIG: Well if you're my mate, you help me out. Mates do things together, so shut up and keep a look out.

BENTLEY: Well, I ain't doing that! No –

CRAIG: Look! . . . You're one of my gang, ain't you, so you do as I tell you. Alright?

BENTLEY: It's stupid. I ain't gonna have nothing to do with it. I'm going home.

CRAIG: Alright, alright, you go then, Derek. You leave your good mate stuck here all on his tod and you know what?

BENTLEY: What?

CRAIG: There just might be a phone call . . . Some nasty little nark might just call the police and tell them Derek Bentley was seen . . . loitering behind the Co-op before it was done.

BENTLEY: Well, I ain't done nothing and I'm going.

CRAIG: You didn't do nothing last time, Derek, but you still got three years.

BENTLEY: Just leave it, Chris, come on, let's go.

CRAIG: You're an ex-con., or good as, they'll really do you this time.

BENTLEY: Look, we . . . we don't have to go in there, we can go somewhere else –

CRAIG: Derek –

BENTLEY: I'll get you some money.

CRAIG: Oh yeah, where?

BENTLEY: I get paid Friday.

CRAIG: Today is Tuesday. Now you've got this nice little job at the furniture shop ain't you, Del? Well, if you want that nice little job tomorrow, you'll come here now and keep a look out.

(CRAIG starts to climb in. BENTLEY keeps watch.)

BENTLEY: Chris –

CRAIG: What?

BENTLEY: Someone's seen me standing here.

CRAIG: Christ! Are they coming this way?

BENTLEY: No.

CRAIG: Well, come in here, then, I need some help forcing this door.

(BENTLEY climbs in after CRAIG. He looks round then disappears

Example 87

from sight. Slide of GODDARD.)

GODDARD (tape): If public opinion gets seriously disturbed by the amount of crime that is prevalent – and I have heard in Court of old people who have dreaded to answer a knock at the door because they don't know what thug may be standing there to take their life savings – there will be a strong tendency for the public to take the law into their own hands. It is time it is realised that crime – and serious crime – has increased in this country to an alarming extent.

Scene Seven

As tape ends, BENTLEY crosses to home area and sits.
MRS BENTLEY enters. Blank slide.

MRS B: Where the hell have you been? Your Dad finished his tea hours ago. You might tell me if you're going to be late. Where've you been?

BENTLEY: Nowhere.

MRS B: What do you mean nowhere? Nowhere's nowhere. Now sit down and eat your tea before it's ruined.

BENTLEY: I don't want nothing.

MRS B: What do you mean, you don't want nothing? Just get it eaten.

BENTLEY: I'm not hungry.

MRS B: Now, come on, Derek. I know I'm angry but that's no reason for you to upset yourself. Just let me know in future that's all. Now let's foget all about it. Eat your tea.

BENTLEY: I can't. I'm not hungry.

MRS B: You're not hungry? That's a turn up for the books.

BENTLEY: Lay off me, mum, will you?

(Pause.)

MRS B: What is it, Derek, what's wrong? What's the matter . . .

BENTLEY: Nothing. I was just thinking.

MRS B: What about?

BENTLEY: Oh, only about some bloke. This bloke I just met.

MRS B: Who? What bloke?

BENTLEY: This Chris Craig bloke.

MRS B: Chris Craig . . . What do you mean, Chris Craig? You don't know him, do you? Derek, do you know Chris Craig?

BENTLEY: Yeah.

'You want to stay away from boys like Craig'.

MRS B: You don't go around with him? Where do you know him from?

BENTLEY: I just know him.

MRS B: You don't bother with him though, do you?

BENTLEY: Well . . . you know . . . I . . . just know him.

MRS B: I've heard terrible things about him. He's no good. You know what he's like, don't you, Derek?

BENTLEY: Yeah, I know what he's like.

MRS B: You want to stay away from boys like him.

BENTLEY: He just follows me around.

MRS B: What do you mean he just follows you around?

BENTLEY: Everywhere I go, he's always there.

MRS B: If he follows you around, you must have something to do with him. Do you have anything to do with Chris Craig?

BENTLEY: No, no, I can't get rid of him.

MRS B: Well, tell him to go away. Keep away from him . . . he's not fit to be on the streets.

BENTLEY: I do tell him to go away, but he's just there all the time.

MRS B: Oh, come on, you're a big lad, and he's only a kid. You can

Example 89

get rid of him if you want to . . . Do you want to, Derek?

BENTLEY: Yes. Course I do.

MRS B: Well, tell him then . . . tell him.

BENTLEY: But he's got a gun . . . he's barmy . . . he's –

MRS B: Got a gun?

BENTLEY: Yeah . . . it's a real gun.

MRS B: Now look, Derek. You've got to get rid of him. You've been to Approved School and you can get into serious trouble being with a boy like that Now stay away.

BENTLEY: I can't stay away from him. He's always at me. Wanting me to do jobs with him.

MRS B: Derek, I'm telling you . . . Keep away from him. I'll see his parents, get this stopped. Is that what's bothering you – getting you upset?

(CRAIG has entered and now knocks on the door.)

MRS B: I'll go. You go upstairs.

(BENTLEY leaves. MRS BENTLEY opens the door. CRAIG stands there.)

MRS B: Er, yes, son, what is it?

CRAIG: Is Del, er Derek, in?

MRS B: Yes, he is, he's upstairs. Who are you?

CRAIG: I'm a mate of his. I wondered if he was coming for a walk.

MRS B: Oh, yes . . . and what's your name?

CRAIG: Chris, Chris Craig.

MRS B: Oh, I see, well, Derek won't be coming out this evening, he's got to help his Dad.

CRAIG: Oh, alright, I'll call another time then.

(He starts to move off.)

MRS B: Just a minute, would you mind hanging on for a while? I'd rather like to have a word with you about Derek. I'd rather you didn't keep calling for him. Just – well, just leave him alone, just for a while.

CRAIG: Why?

MRS B: Now, you know why. You've been pestering him, haven't you?

CRAIG: Is that what he said?

MRS B: Look, I don't want to go into that, I'm just asking you to keep away for a bit, that's all. I'm sure you've got plenty of other friends. I mean, Derek, he's well, I know you're younger than Derek and he's . . . he's older than you, but . . . you're a very smart lad.

CRAIG: Thank you.

MRS B: Yeah, well, Derek's not quite so good at looking after himself.

CRAIG: But I look out for him, Mrs Bentley.

MRS B: Yes, I'm sure you do, but that's not quite good enough is it? He's been in trouble before, and . . . well . . .

CRAIG: Yes, I know.

MRS B: *You* should understand then. Cos he's got a smashing job now, and I don't want any bother, I know the sort of things you get up to, Chris, you and your friends, . . . and I don't want our Derek involved.

CRAIG: It's only fun, Mrs Bentley.

MRS B: I don't care what you call it, I'm not having our Derek getting mixed up in it . . . in . . . in your games. So I've told you, and that's final.

CRAIG: You think I'm dangerous, don't you? Eh?

MRS B: I think you're playing at being dangerous, yes. But —

CRAIG (suddenly pulling out knuckleduster): I'm not playin', lady, so you'd better watch what you say about me, and your Derek had better watch, cos otherwise you might find out just how serious I am.

Craig threatens Mrs. Bentley.

Example 91

(Pause. CRAIG pulls himself together.)

Just a joke, Mrs Bentley. I hope I didn't frighten you. Like you said, I was just playing. Tell your Derek, I'll be seeing him. Bye, bye.

(He leaves, whistling. MRS BENTLEY stands horror-struck. BENTLEY re-enters.)

BENTLEY: Has he gone, Mum? Did you get rid of him alright? Will he leave me alone now? (Pause.) Mum? Did he say he wouldn't bother me no more? . . . What did he say, Mum. (Pause.) What happened?

MRS B: I . . . I . . . there's just one way of sorting out that young . . . there's just one way, and I'm going right now, and I'm going to do it.

Scene Eight

She moves to Police Station and hammers on desk. BENTLEY remains on. SERGEANT FAIRFAX comes on. Slide of FAIRFAX.

FAIRFAX: Can I help you, love?

MRS B: Well, somebody's got to help me. If an ordinary person can't walk down the street without being bothered by young hooligans, I don't . . .

FAIRFAX: Calm down, love, calm down. Now, just give me your name.

MRS B: Bentley, Mrs Lillian Bentley.

FAIRFAX (writing in the desk book): Is that 'EY'?

MRS B: Yes, of course, it's 'EY'.

FAIRFAX: Address, love?

MRS B: Number One, Fairview Road, Norbury.

FAIRFAX: Now then, what's it all about?

MRS B: I've told you, officer. There's a young lad bothering my son. He's a bad type. He's a troublemaker. I want him kept away from my Derek.

FAIRFAX: What's he done?

MRS B: Nothing – yet. But I know something's going to happen if we don't stop it now.

FAIRFAX: Alright – give us details and we'll see what we can do. What's this lad's name?

MRS B: Craig, Christopher Craig.

FAIRFAX: Chris Craig, oh yes, he is a bit of a troublemaker, isn't he . . .

MRS B: Yes, he is. So what are you going to do about keeping him away from Derek?

FAIRFAX: Well, we'll keep an eye on him of course. My advice to you is to tell your son to ignore him, Mrs Bentley, just ignore him.

MRS B: But he won't go away!

FAIRFAX: Look, I've told you we'll keep an eye on him, love, but until he breaks the law that's all we can do.

(Starts to move away, turns and sees MRS BENTLEY still standing there.)

Sorry, love.

(He leaves. Blank slide.)

MRS B (under breath, as she returns home): Oh, for crying out loud . . .

BENTLEY: Where've you been, Mum?

MRS B: The Police Station.

BENTLEY: What for?

MRS B: To get rid of that Craig boy of course!

BENTLEY: You shouldn't have done that!

MRS B: Fat lot of good it did. Don't worry, Derek, we'll keep him away from you. Me, and your Dad, if anyone comes to the door, we'll answer it, and you can go up to your room. We'll keep Chris Craig away from you. Don't worry.

(Both freeze.)

Scene Nine

CRAIG enters laughing followed by a worried NORMAN PARSLEY.

CRAIG: Did you see that old geezer when I made him put that fruit on his head? Laugh? 'Kiss my feet,' I says, 'before I blow your brains out, grandad.' Legs Diamond couldn't't've done it better. (Laughs.) How much did we get?

PARSLEY: What?

CRAIG: Are you asleep, Norman, I said, 'How much did we get?'

PARSLEY: Oh, er seven . . . seven quid and a ring.

CRAIG: Chicken feed. You know, I'm sick of these little jobs, I mean, it's a good laugh, but it's the same old risks, and what do you get? Peanuts! It's about time we got a bit more ambitious.

PARSLEY: I think . . . sometimes, I think you, er we, we take more risks than we should — than we need, I mean.

CRAIG: Are you talking about tonight, Norman, are you saying I'm not so clever?

Example 93

PARSLEY: No, Chris, I'm not saying that.

CRAIG: That's good. I mean, you've got to have a laugh, ain't ya? (Laughs.) I hope my little Norman Parsley ain't losing his sense of humour, cos I got this great job lined up tomorrow and I need his help, see?

PARSLEY: I thought we might . . .

CRAIG: You, Norman, thinking?

PARSLEY: No, no, Chris, it's nothing.

CRAIG: Come on, Norman, don't be shy, if you've been thinking, I want to know about it.

PARSLEY: Well, it's nothing . . . it's just, I thought we might lay off for a bit.

CRAIG: Lay off?

PARSLEY: Yeah, I thought, after tonight, we might, you know, lie low . . . for a bit.

CRAIG: You shouldn't do it, son.

PARSLEY (frightened): What?

CRAIG: Think.

PARSLEY: Oh yeah. (Weak laugh.)

(Pause.)

CRAIG: I hope my little sage and parsley ain't turning yellow on me.

PARSLEY: No, no, it's not that. It's just we ought to rest it a bit, I mean that old geezer, say you, we . . . we don't want to get caught, do we?

CRAIG (pulling out gun and becoming manic): They ain't never gonna catch me. The bastards sent my brother down for twelve years and they're gonna pay for that, all of them, ain't no one gonna take Chris Craig, not alive at any rate, no way!

(Pause. He calms down again.)

So you stick with me, Norman, I'll look after you, mate.

PARSLEY: Yeah, thanks, Chris.

CRAIG: 'S alright. I'll see you at the bus station then, tomorrow tea-time. (Pause.) I will see you, won't I, Norman?

PARSLEY (desperate): Oh . . . . er, eh, Chris, I've just remembered, you'r never going to believe this.

CRAIG: Try me.

PARSLEY: It's my Grandad. He's coming up tomorrow from er . . . from Bristol, that's it, coming up special to see me, so I won't be able to come.

CRAIG: That right?

Craig intimidates Parsley.

PARSLEY: Yeah, yeah, honest, Chris, I'd forgotten all about it, but it's the truth, honest it is.

(He is almost in tears.)

CRAIG: I believe you, Norman. I'll believe anybody. Once. I know you'd never cross me (Indicating gun.) don't I?

PARSLEY: Yeah, yeah. I'd better be going now, Chris.

(He starts to move off.)

CRAIG: Wait a minute, my old mate. I mean, seeing as you can't do the job yourself, you'd better get me someone else who can, ain't ya?

PARSLEY: Yeah, sure, Chris, anything you like. Who? Who do you want?

CRAIG: Derek Bentley.

(PARSLEY goes. CRAIG remains on.)

Scene Ten

Sound effect of television. MRS BENTLEY turns to DEREK.

MRS B: You'll have to switch that thing off when your Dad comes home, 'cos he'll want you to give him a hand in the workshop.

Example 95

BENTLEY: Alright, Mum.

(Knock at door. They exchange glances. She goes and returns.)

MRS B: All clear! It's not Craig at all. It's a boy called Norman Parsley. He seems a nice lad, very well spoken.

BENTLEY: Did you tell him I was out?

MRS B: Didn't seem much point.

BENTLEY: So he knows that I'm here?

MRS B: Oh yes. He'd like you to go for a walk with him. Can't be much harm in that if you want to go.

(PARSLEY has appeared behind MRS BENTLEY and over her heads signals to BENTLEY what will happen if he doesn't come.)

BENTLEY: Hello, Norman.

PARSLEY: Are you coming?

BENTLEY: Yeah. I won't be long, Mum.

MRS B: Alright, Derek. Take care.

(She turns off TV and leaves.)

Scene Eleven

CRAIG waiting. PARSLEY brings BENTLEY to him.

PARSLEY: Here he is, Chris.

CRAIG: See you, Norman.

PARSLEY: See you.

(He leaves.)

BENTLEY: See you, Norman.

CRAIG: Hi, Del, long time no see.

BENTLEY: Yeah.

CRAIG: I've missed you. Nice to see you again.

(Pause. BENTLEY relaxes.)

BENTLEY: Well, what are we going to do tonight, then?

CRAIG: Thought we'd go down to Croydon. Look round the shops, have a coffee. What d'you reckon, Del?

BENTLEY: Yeah. OK, Kiddo.

CRAIG: Great . . . Oh, Del, I've got a present for you.

(He slips it into BENTLEY's pocket. BENTLEY takes it out and looks at it. It's a knuckleduster.)

Don't tell me you don't want it.

(BENTLEY is about to protest when there is the sound of a bus approaching.)

Here's the bus! Come on, Del, we're going to miss it.

(They rush off.)

(Sound of phone ringing on tape then the following recorded dialogue:)

FAIRFAX: Croydon Police Station.

WOMAN: Hello, my name's Mrs Ware of Tamworth Road, Croydon.

FAIRFAX: Yes, madam.

WOMAN: I think there's something up. My daughter's spotted two men on the roof of the warehouse opposite.

(Slide of rooftop.)

We think they're trying to break in. My daughter saw them climbing up.

FAIRFAX: How long have they been there?

WOMAN: They've only just reached the top. I think you should hurry.

FAIRFAX: We'll be right over. What number are you?

WOMAN: 74.

Scene Twelve

As the tape is ending, CRAIG climbs on to the roof.

CRAIG: Come on, Derek, you're not bloody paralysed. You stay on that drainpipe much longer, people'll think you're a bloody cat.

BENTLEY (off): My coat's stuck.

CRAIG: Come *on*.

(BENTLEY appears and they look round the rooftop as FAIRFAX's recorded voice is heard.)

FAIRFAX (tape): Sergeant Fairfax, Croydon Police. At 9.15 p.m. on 2nd November, 1952, suspects were reported on the roof of a warehouse in Tamworth Road, Croydon. We immediately got into a police van and proceeded to the premises in question. Police Car 7Z patrolling the streets of Croydon was also alerted, and the two vehicles arrived at the scene at almost exactly the same time . . .

(Sound of cars pulling up. CRAIG and BENTLEY react and hide behind the stack at far end of roof. Voice on tape continues.)

Around 9.20 p.m. P.C. Miles, driver of the patrol car, was sent to fetch the keys to the door that leads to the roof. I now began to climb up onto the roof to investigate.

(FAIRFAX enters with a torch.)

The roof was long and flat, approximately 54 feet by 90 feet.

Example 97

At one end, the roof entrance, at the other, the head of the lift shaft. (He uses the torch to indicate this.) The roof was 30 feet above the ground. We knew that the only entrance on to the roof was locked. (He checks door.) When the two youths heard the cars pull up, they must have tried to hide. Visibility was poor but there was only one place they could be. (He shines torch at lift shaft.) I was about some twenty feet from the lift shaft when I called out . . .

FAIRFAX (live): I'm a Police Officer. Come out from behind that stack!

FAIRFAX (tape): Craig shouted back . . .

CRAIG: If you want us, come and get us.

FAIRFAX (tape): There was a pause and I advanced towards the lift shaft . . . (The sequence is acted out.) I heard Bentley say . . .

BENTLEY: I've had enough.

FAIRFAX (tape): He emerged from hiding and I grabbed him. I then took Bentley round the stack with a view to closing in on Craig. We came face to face with him.

(All freeze on stage. Voice on tape continues fast.)

Bentley then broke away from me and as he did so shouted, 'Let him have it Chris.' There was a loud bang and a flash, and something hit my shoulder.

(All these things now happen together. CRAIG aims wildly. BENTLEY and FAIRFAX separate. It's not clear whether BENTLEY has pulled away or not or whether he has said anything. FAIRFAX falls to the ground and BENTLEY moves to him. No sound.)

I fell to the ground. Bentley asked me if I was alright. His voice jerked me back to consciousness. I jumped to my feet and shouted to the men below . . .

FAIRFAX (live): They've got guns! Get the place surrounded!

FAIRFAX (tape): Craig fired again but missed completely. Bentley was still standing where I had fallen, and he shouted to Craig . . .

BENTLEY: You bloody fool.

FAIRFAX (tape): I pulled him behind the cover of the roof entrance. He then produced a knuckleduster from his pocket and handed it over to me, saying . . .

BENTLEY: That's all I've got, guv'nor, I haven't got a gun.

FAIRFAX (tape): We waited. Eventually, I called out to Craig . . .

FAIRFAX (live): Drop your gun!

FAIRFAX (tape): He shouted back defiantly . . .

CRAIG (by now very panicky): Come and get it.

FAIRFAX (tape): We still waited. Below, a crowd had gathered and more police arrived, including armed police marksmen who were moving into position. Everywhere there was chaos and confusion. (Sound effects.) Some ten minutes passed in this way. Then there was a new sound. (Sound of footsteps, keys jangling.) P.C. Miles had collected the keys and was coming up the staircase that led on to the roof. The door did not open easily and he had to push against it. (Sound effects.) I warned him to be careful. Then . . . he burst through the door and on to the roof top.

(MILES bursts in. He faces CRAIG. CRAIG fires. A real blank this time so the bang is heard. MILES falls. All freeze.)

NARRATOR (enters): We'll take a short break now. See you in twenty minutes.

End of Part One. All clear from stage.

Part Two

Scene One

As audience returns, the slide of the Daily Mail front page reporting the shooting is up. Then blank slide. FAIRFAX, one arm in sling, hustles BENTLEY into middle of stage and sits him down. He holds BENTLEY's statement. While they are entering, voices are heard off arguing. MRS BENTLEY is demanding to be allowed to see her son, a Police Officer tells her she can't.

MRS B (off): I want to see my boy. Where's my boy? What are you doing with him? I've got to know what's happening.

(She has entered and reached the desk. FAIRFAX leaves BENTLEY and goes to her.)

FAIRFAX: What the hell's going on? Who are you?

MRS B: Mrs Lillian Bentley. You're holding my son, Derek. I want to see him. I've got to see him. You've got no right to hold him here.

(Pause.)

FAIRFAX: Listen, missus. We have got your son. Just go home, please. You can see him in the morning.

MRS B: I want to know what's going on. All I know is that the police came to my house, charged through it throwing things about, and took a knife away. They said Derek's killed a man. That can't be true.

FAIRFAX: A policeman has been killed. Now do as I say, Mrs Bentley, go home.

Example 99

MRS B: I can't, and you can't do things like this.

FAIRFAX: Just go home, Mrs Bentley, *please.*

MRS B: I demand to see him and I demand to know what's going on. How do you think I feel seeing my son treated this way?

FAIRFAX (finally losing control): How do you think *I* feel? One of my mates has just been shot, Mrs Bentley. And he's got a wife, Mrs Bentley and somebody's got to tell her her husband's dead. And all because some stupid little bastard decides he's going to act big. So why don't you think what I feel, Mrs Bentley? And I can't go and complain to somebody about it, Mrs Bentley, it's not allowed.

(Pause.)

Do me a favour, missus, go home.

(MRS BENTLEY leaves. FAIRFAX returns to taking BENTLEY's statement.)

FAIRFAX (wearily): Alright, where were we?

BENTLEY: What happened to Chris?

FAIRFAX: He threw himself off the roof.

BENTLEY: Is he dead?

(Pause.)

FAIRFAX: No . . . Now then. (Reads statement.) "A little later, the door opened and a policeman in uniform came out. Chris fired again then and this policeman fell down. I could see he was hurt as a lot of blood came from his forehead just above his nose. The policeman dragged him round the corner behind the brickwork entrance to the door. I remember I shouted something but I forget what it was. The policeman then pushed me down the stairs and I did not see any more. I knew we were going to break into the place, I did not know what we were going to get — just anything that was going. I did not have a gun and I did not know Chris had one until he shot. I now know that the policeman in uniform is dead."

(Pause. BENTLEY has sat there in a daze.)

"This statement has been read to me and is true . . ." (handing statement and pen to Bentley.) Sign it!

(Pause.)

BENTLEY: I can't.

FAIRFAX: What?

BENTLEY: I can't write!

(Pause.)

FAIRFAX (suppressing anger): Can you make letters?

Bentley signs
his statement.

BENTLEY: Yes.

FAIRFAX: Right. Copy these. D . . E . . R . . E . . K . . . .

(The tape comes on. During the tape, BENTLEY finishes the signing and FAIRFAX exits with the statement.)

NARRATOR (tape): On 11th November, Christopher Craig appeared for the first time in public. He was being carried on a stretcher into Croydon Magistrates Court when he was attacked by an angry crowd. There were shouts of "He ought to swing," and "Let's get hold of the dirty bastard and choke him." He was only saved from physical attack by the police, all colleagues of the dead policeman. On 18th November, Craig and Bentley appeared together for the first time and were charged with the attempted murder of Sergeant Fairfax as well as the murder of P.C. Miles. Both pleaded not guilty, and were granted legal aid to arrange their defences.

Scene Two

CASSELS enters. Slide of CASSELS fading later to blank side.

CASSELS: Derek William Bentley? (BENTLEY looks up.) My name's Cassels. I'm your defending counsel. You do understand what that

Example 101

is, don't you? It's my job to say what can be said in your favour in Court. (Looking through papers.) Though heaven knows it's not going to be an easy job. You've really become quite famous, Bentley, being charged with murdering a policeman.

BENTLEY: But Chris did it. He shot him.

CASSELS: I'm afraid, Bentley, it's not as simple as that. You were involved. You agreed to go with Chris on a robbery. You yourself carried a weapon.

BENTLEY: He gave me that.

CASSELS: Nevertheless, you carried a weapon, Bentley, and you went off on a robbery with Craig and during the course of that robbery he shot a policeman. We're up against a very sharp Prosecution Counsel who'll be out to prove that the two of you agreed to use violence if you were apprehended in the course of your robbery . . .

BENTLEY: But —

CASSELS: Perhaps you would be good enough to let me finish. If that agreement could be proved, then it would mean that you were involved in the murder, although you didn't fire the gun which killed the policeman. Did you know he was armed?

BENTLEY: But Chris . . . well, he always had guns, but that night . . . he . . .

CASSELS: Come along, Bentley, you'll have to be a bit clearer than that in Court. I don't know whether it's occurred to you, Bentley, but if you're found guilty, you could hang. —

BENTLEY: It was Chris, Chris who —

CASSELS: Bentley, Craig is only 16. The law does not allow a boy of under 18 to be hung. Bentley, it may need me to point out to you that though Craig is 16, you are 19. (Pause.) So please bend your mind to getting *some* things clear in your head. (Looks at papers.) Now, it says here that on the night in question you came out from hiding and came towards Police Sergeant Fairfax to give yourself up.

BENTLEY: He arrested me.

CASSELS: Did he say so?

BENTLEY: He didn't say anything.

CASSELS: But he took hold of you?

BENTLEY: Yes.

CASSELS: And he stayed holding you?

BENTLEY: Yes . . . well, not all the time.

CASSELS: But you're certain he arrested you?

BENTLEY: Yes.

CASSELS: And you were under arrest when the fatal shot was fired?

BENTLEY: Yes.

CASSELS: Good. That's important, Bentley, remember it.

BENTLEY: Yes.

CASSELS (throwing him a grey tie): And I want you to wear this in Court, not the one you're wearing now. And remember to speak up and be as clear as you can. You must call the Judge "My Lord" and everyone else "Sir". Understand?

BENTLEY: Yes.

CASSELS: Good. See you in Court, Bentley.

(Exit CASSELS. BENTLEY sets chair for Court and goes.)

Scene Three

Sound of general hubbub. HARRY PROCTER enters.

PROCTER: Ello, ello, ello, Harry Procter, reporter, *Sunday Pictorial*. Gawd, crowded in here, ain't it? Still I suppose we're lucky to get in here at all. Do you know they're fighting for tickets outside? Crazy, ain't it? Tickets for a trial. It's these bloody spivs, make money out of anything they could. Thirty quid a ticket, that's the going price. Still, should be a good show though.

(HUMPHRIES crosses the stage and starts talking to CASSELS.)

See that — Prosecuting Counsel, Christmas Humphries. Wouldn't like to wake up in the morning and find that in my stocking. Wouldn't fancy being in Craig and Bentley's shoes either. You know who the judge is? Head of the hang 'em and flog 'em brigade himself, Lord Chief Justice Goddard.

(PROCTER stands aside. BENTLEY goes to witness box. GODDARD enters and seats himself. Slide: "The trial, second day: Case for the defence".)

GODDARD: Continue, Mr Cassels.

CASSELS: When you got to the roof what happened then?

BENTLEY: Some lights in the garden. Someone shone a light in the garden, and so we got behind a stack or lift shaft.

CASSELS: Did Craig say something to you at that time?

BENTLEY: Yes, sir. He said 'Get behind here.'

CASSELS: Did you know at that time that he had got a gun?

BENTLEY: No, sir.

CASSELS: What happened after you got behind the stack?

BENTLEY: Sergeant Fairfax come and took me, sir, because I could not see nothing where I was standing and he come and took me and walked me across the roof.

Example 103

Cassels, defending counsel, interviews Bentley.

CASSELS: When Sergeant Fairfax came and took you, did he say anything?

BENTLEY: He said "I'm a police officer, I've got the place surrounded."

CASSELS: When Sergeant Fairfax took hold of you, did you make any effort to struggle?

BENTLEY: No, sir.

CASSELS: Or any attempt to strike him?

BENTLEY: No.

CASSELS: At the time when Sergeant Fairfax took hold of you, did you know that Craig was armed?

BENTLEY: No, sir.

CASSELS: Did you say anything before any shot was fired?

BENTLEY: No.

CASSELS: What had happened between the time Sergeant Fairfax took hold of you and the time the first shot was fired?

BENTLEY: Well, I don't know what happened on Christopher's side, sir, but Sergeant Fairfax had me and nothing happened.

CASSELS: Did you break away from him once?

BENTLEY: No sir.

CASSELS: Did you say, "Let him have it, Chris."?

BENTLEY: No, sir.

CASSELS: What happened when the shot was fired?

BENTLEY: Sergeant Fairfax leaned on me and fell over like *that*. He did not touch the floor though.

CASSELS: What did you do when the shot was fired?

BENTLEY: I stood by Sergeant Fairfax.

CASSELS: You stood by Sergeant Fairfax?

BENTLEY: Yes, sir.

CASSELS: Did you make any attempt to get away from him?

BENTLEY: No, sir.

CASSELS: Did you make any attempt to strike him while he was on the ground or while he was falling?

BENTLEY: No.

CASSELS: Did you make any attempt to join Craig?

BENTLEY: No, sir.

CASSELS: What happened when Sergeant Fairfax recovered from the shock?

BENTLEY: He got up – well, leaned up – and put me behind that staircase.

CASSELS: Did you make any attempt to get away from him?

BENTLEY: No, sir.

CASSELS: Is it right, as he says, that he searched you and found the knuckleduster?

BENTLEY: I gave him the knuckleduster. I took it out of my pocket myself.

CASSELS: From that time until you were taken downstairs by the police, did you remain behind the staircase head?

BENTLEY: I did.

CASSELS: Were you being held all the time by police officers?

BENTLEY: No, sir.

CASSELS: Was there anyone to prevent you if you had wanted to join Craig?

BENTLEY: No, sir.

CASSELS: Your witness, Mr Humphries.

(CASSELS sits. HUMPHRIES rises, holding BENTLEY's statement.)

Example 105

HUMPHRIES: Look at your statement, Exhibit No 15, will you?

BENTLEY: It's no good me looking at that, sir.

GODDARD: He cannot read it.

HUMPHRIES: I shall read to you a few lines from the end.
"I knew we were going to break into the place. I did not know what we were going to get — just anything that was going."
Was that statement written down and read over to you?

BENTLEY: Yes, sir.

HUMPHRIES: And you signed the statement as true?

BENTLEY: Yes, sir.

HUMPHRIES: Did you say it?

BENTLEY: No, sir.

HUMPHRIES: Then why did you sign the statement as true when it was read over to you?

BENTLEY: Because I did not know what I was signing.

GODDARD: You did not know what you were signing?

BENTLEY: I can't remember all that I say.

HUMPHRIES: The evidence is that that statement — and it is not very long — was read over to you and then you signed it or tried to sign it. You needed some help but in the end you signed it as true?

BENTLEY: Yes.

Christmas Humphries cross-examines.

HUMPHRIES: Well, did you say it or not?

BENTLEY: No, sir.

HUMPHRIES: What are you suggesting then – that a police officer writes down something you did not say when he has sworn he wrote down what you said?

BENTLEY: Not right then.

HUMPHRIES: The moment the police came out to you you knew they were police?

BENTLEY: He called out and said so.

HUMPHRIES: Then he grabbed you?

BENTLEY: Yes.

HUMPHRIES: And you knew you were grabbed by a police officer when you were trying to commit a crime – arrested? You know what that means?

BENTLEY: Yes.

HUMPHRIES: And while you were arrested you do your best to break away and he, with you in custody, pursues Craig round the stack. Is that right?

BENTLEY: No, sir.

HUMPHRIES: At any rate, you broke away from him did you not?

BENTLEY: No, sir.

HUMPHRIES: And when he is no longer holding you, you call out "Let him have it, Chris"?

BENTLEY: No, sir.

HUMPHRIES: So all the officers who heard you say that are wrong are they?

BENTLEY: That is right.

HUMPHRIES: And in fact Chris did let him have it?

BENTLEY: He did shoot, sir.

HUMPHRIES: Did you shout anything out to Chris when he was shooting?

BENTLEY: Not as far as I can remember, sir.

HUMPHRIES: You did nothing to stop him shooting further did you?

BENTLEY: To stop Craig, sir?

HUMPHRIES: Yes.

BENTLEY: That would be silly, wouldn't it, sir?

HUMPHRIES: Why?

Example 107

BENTLEY: That would have been silly. His mind must have been disturbed.

HUMPHRIES: When he shot, you thought his mind must have been disturbed, and it was not worth while telling him to stop?

BENTLEY: If I had got in his way he might have shot me, sir.

GODDARD: Never mind about getting in his way. You did not shout out, "Let him have it, Chris." Did you shout out "For God's sake don't fire" or "Shut up doing that" at any one of those shots?

BENTLEY: I cannot remember, sir.

HUMPHRIES: According to you, when you were over by the staircase head you were not being held by the police officer. Is that right?

BENTLEY: That is right.

HUMPHRIES: So that you were not under arrest at the time?

BENTLEY: I was standing there, sir.

HUMPHRIES: But you were not being held?

BENTLEY: No.

HUMPHRIES: You were quite free to run if you wanted to?

BENTLEY: Yes.

HUMPHRIES: And you were still on the roof when the shooting was going on?

BENTLEY: Yes.

HUMPHRIES: Your mind was still with Craig was it not?

BENTLEY: No, sir.

HUMPHRIES: You were doing nothing to stop him doing what you had come up to do together — break in?

BENTLEY: We had come up to break in, not to kill, sir.

HUMPHRIES: In fact, you incited him to do something further; you shouted out, 'Look out Chris; they're taking me down'?

BENTLEY: That was in case he shot me, sir.

HUMPHRIES: You were only thinking of your own skin you mean?

BENTLEY: If he shot me, there was another police officer with me.

HUMPHRIES: Ah, you were frightened he might shoot at the police and hit you by mistake?

BENTLEY: He might hit anybody.

HUMPHRIES: The police did not matter! You knew he was a thoroughly dangerous and irresponsible person with a gun in his hand, did you not?

BENTLEY: At the time when he was shooting, yes, sir.

HUMPHRIES: And well before you got on the roof?

BENTLEY: No, sir.

HUMPHRIES: And when you thought you were being taken down you incited him to shoot further so that you might get away from the police?

BENTLEY: If I had done as you say, sir, I might have been shot myself.

HUMPHRIES: I see – still thinking of your own skin. In other words, you were prepared to assist Craig by such hitting with knuckledusters or shooting with a revolver at the police as would enable you to escape if caught in the crime that you were committing?

BENTLEY: No, sir.

CASSELS: My Lord, that is the case for Bentley.

(HUMPHRIES and CASSELS sit.)

GODDARD: Stand down, Bentley.

(BENTLEY moves to the dock. Slide: "Trial third day: Lord GODDARD's summing up.")

GODDARD: Now members of the jury, in many respects this is a very terrible case and it is one therefore that it is desirable you and I approach in as calm a frame of mind as we can. Here two lads, one of 16 and one of 19, *admittedly* out on a shop-breaking expedition at night, and the result is that a young policeman, while in the execution of his duty, is shot dead.

The defence of the prisoner, Craig, is that he asks you to reduce the charge to manslaughter. Now, manslaughter can only be accepted here if you think that the whole thing is accidental. How it can be said to be accidental, I confess, seems to me to be exceedingly difficult.

In the case of Bentley, the defence is: I did not know he had a gun, and I deny that I said, "Let him have it, Chris!" The first thing you have got to consider is whether or not he knew Craig was armed. Craig himself has said in Court that he carried a revolver for the purpose of boasting and making himself a big man. Can you suppose for a moment that he would not have told his pals that he had got a revolver? I should think you would come to the conclusion that almost the first thing Craig would tell Bentley if they were going off on a shop-breaking expedition would be, 'It's alright, I've got a revolver with me.'

Then see what Bentley had with him. Where is that knuckleduster? (It is handed to him.) Apparently it was given to him by Craig, but Bentley was armed with this knuckleduster. Have you ever seen a more horrible sort of weapon? This is to hit a person in the face. You grasp it here, your fingers go through, and you can kill a

Example 109

person with this. Of course if the blow with the steel is not enough, you have got this spike in the side to jab. It is a shocking weapon. Can you believe for a moment Bentley did not know Craig had a gun?

Then of course the most serious piece of evidence against Bentley is that he called out to Craig: "Let him have it, Chris!" and then the firing began and the very first shot struck an officer. Three police officers in all swear that they heard Bentley call that out. The police officers that night showed the highest gallantry. They were conspicuously brave. Are you going to say that they are conspicuous liars?

I started by saying this was a dreadful case. It is dreadful to think that two lads, coming from decent homes, should with weapons like this, go out to break the law and finish by shooting policemen. (Hands back knuckleduster.)

With these words I will ask you to go to the serious and solemn duty that you have of considering your verdict.

(Pause. Slide: "The verdict". CRAIG stands by BENTLEY in the dock. Enter FOREMAN of the Jury.)

GODDARD: Members of the jury, are you agreed upon your verdict?

FOREMAN: We are.

GODDARD: Do you find the prisoner Christopher Craig guilty or not guilty of murder?

FOREMAN: Guilty.

GODDARD: Do you find the prisoner Derek William Bentley guilty or not guilty of murder?

FOREMAN: Guilty, with a recommendation to mercy.

GODDARD: Christopher Craig, you stand convicted of murder, have you anything to say why sentence should not be passed according to law? (Pause.) Derek William Bentley, you stand convicted of murder, have you anything to say why sentence should not be passed according to law?

Christopher Craig, you are under eighteen, but in my judgment and evidently in the judgment of the jury, you are the more guilty of the two. Your heart was filled with hate, and you murdered a policeman without thought of his wife, his family or himself; and never once have you expressed a word of sorrow for what you have done. I shall tell the Secretary of State when forwarding the recommendation of the jury in Bentley's case that in my opinion you are one of the most dangerous criminals who has ever stood in that dock. The sentence upon you is that you be kept in strict custody until the pleasure of Her Majesty be known. Take him down.

(CRAIG stands down.)

Derek William Bentley, you are nineteen years of age. It is my duty to pass upon you the only sentence which the law can pass for the crime of wilful murder. The sentence of the Court upon you is that you be taken from this place to a lawful prison, and thence to a place of execution, and there you suffer death by hanging, and that your body be buried within the precincts of the prison in which you shall have been last confined before your execution; and may the Lord have mercy upon your soul. Take him down.

(BENTLEY stands down. The Court leaves. Blank slide. PROCTER comes forward.)

PROCTER: Well, how about that then eh? What a trial. Better'n Billy Smart's Circus ain't it? Christmas Humphries and his Performing Hooligans. Well, you see old Goddard with that knuckleduster? Wouldn't like to meet him on a dark night, eh? And the whole thing over in two and a half days. Ten hours the lot. I've spent longer waiting for a 22 bus. Anyway, one thing's for certain, after that verdict, it won't be Craig that people want to hear about any more. No, all eyes'll be going on Bentley. Mine included.

(CASSELS crosses the stage looking at papers. MRS BENTLEY rushes after him.)

PROCTER: Mrs Bentley, Mrs Bentley, could you say a few words?

MRS B: Mr Cassels, Mr Cassels —

CASSELS (still busy with papers): Yes, Mrs Bentley, what is it?

MRS B: I don't get it. What's happened? What are they going to do to Derek?

PROCTER (eavesdropping): Good question.

CASSELS (freezing him with a stare): Excuse me, my man.

(CASSELS leads MRS BENTLEY away to another part of stage.)

CASSELS: Now, Mrs Bentley, what is it?

MRS B: Please tell me what's going to happen? Now they've sentenced Derek to death I —

CASSELS: There's no point in getting agitated, Mrs Bentley. Now that Craig's out of the way, Bentley has a very reasonable case for appealing against sentence. And that is what I intend to do, appeal.

MRS B: But will it be the same judge?

CASSELS: No, no, Mrs Bentley, there'll be a different judge. An appeal judge called Croom-Johnson.

MRS B: But what will happen, will he hear the case all over again? Will he —

Example 111

CASSELS: I think you'd better let me explain, Mrs Bentley. In the case that's just been heard the facts, the things that happened to your son and his companion, were examined. In the Appeal Court we look at the Court's decision from a legal point of view.

MRS B: But they said nothing about his illnesses, about —

CASSELS: Mrs Bentley, we are dealing now with important points of law, and they are really best left to those who understand them. Do you understand?

MRS B (resigned): Yes.

CASSELS: Rest assured, I will put your son's case just as well then as I did today. Good day, madam.

(Exit CASSELS. MRS BENTLEY turns to go.)

PROCTER: Mrs Bentley, Mrs Bentley —

MRS B: Please, not now.

(She leaves.)

PROCTER: Oh well, suit yourself. We've all got a job to do, missus. (Consults notepad.) Ah, well, I shouldn't think that Cassels can be too serious about an appeal. I mean, after all, Goddard is the Lord Chief Justice, ain't he, the boss of all the judges. So, I don't somehow reckon that this Croom-Johnson's going to say that his Lordship muched the trial up. I mean you don't rat on your boss publicly, do you, specially if you get paid as much as Croom-Johnson does.

Scene Four

Slide: "The Appeal: Presiding Judge CROOM-JOHNSON."
PROCTER leaves. Enter CROOM-JOHNSON, who sits, and CASSELS.

CASSELS: My lord, appeal is made on two grounds. Firstly, that Lord Goddard's summing-up of Bentley's case was not totally adequate and left out some important information relevant to Bentley's case.

CROOM: In the opinion of the Court, the idea that there was a failure on the part of the Lord Chief Justice to say anything short of what was required in putting that sort of a case to the jury is entirely wrong.

CASSELS: The second point is that the jury should have been told to consider when the joint adventure of the two youths stopped being a joint adventure.

CROOM: What on earth do you mean?

CASSELS: Bentley was already under arrest for fifteen minutes before PC Miles was shot. He gave himself up and made no attempt to escape. This was a highly important fact that Lord Goddard should have mentioned in his summing-up.

CROOM: Surely a judge in the course of summing-up a criminal trial
cannot deal with every little point – the judge must be allowed a
little latitude mustn't he?

CASSELS: But in the police statement by Bentley and in the police
evidence in court and even in the opening remarks of my learned
colleague, Mr Humphries, the fact that Bentley was under arrest
was admitted, I would respectfully point out.

CROOM: Unfortunately Bentley was asked specifically at the hearing
whether he was under arrest or not at the time when the shot that
killed Miles was fired. He would not have it. He said that he had
not been arrested, that he was not under arrest, that the police
officer had not detained him and all the rest of it. In the face of
that, it seems that it is idle to suggest that this point, if it be the
point, is one which the jury could have taken into consideration
and about which the Chief Justice ought to have directed the jury.
Appeal dismissed.

(Exit CROOM-JOHNSON. Blank slide.)

CASSELS: Personally, I think both the little bastards ought to swing.

(Exit CASSELS. Enter PROCTER.)

PROCTER: There you go. Didn't take long did it? All over in under an
hour. And leaving me with a good story line to find. I reckon it's.
the family – weeping Mum, anxious father, puzzled little
brothers and sisters, faithful doggie on the hearth rug. Could be
great. And only fifteen days to go before Derek gets topped.

Scene Five

PROCTER crosses stage as if to BENTLEY home, finds door open,
enters and starts taking photos. MRS BENTLEY comes in. He
notices her.

PROCTER: Excuse me, Mrs Bentley, er Harry Procter, Sunday
Pictorial. How do you feel now the Appeal's been rejected?
It must be quite a blow to your family's hopes, Mrs Bentley.

MRS B: Yes, I don't understand, I don't believe it. How could they?
Derek never fired that gun. We thought it would be alright.

PROCTER: Er, how many are there in your family, Mrs Bentley?

(He pulls out his pad.)

MRS B: My husband, myself, Iris – that's my daughter – and Denis,
my youngest boy.

PROCTER: Any pets?

MRS B: Well there's Derek's dog and – what the hell have they got
to do with it?

Example 113

An interview with Mrs. Bentley.

PROCTER: And they're all thunderstruck by this blow, Mrs Bentley?
Is it true that Derek suffers from epilepsy?

MRS B: Yes, yes, it is.

PROCTER: And how about the neighbours, any trouble with them?
You know bricks through the windows, threatening letters,
anything like that?

MRS B: Oh ńo, no. Not any more.

PROCTER: You mean you have had bricks through your windows,
Mrs Bentley?

MRS B: No I don't mean . . . there are so many kind letters now.

PROCTER: Letters . . . letters of support?

MRS B: Letters saying it's wrong for Derek to hang.

PROCTER: And who are these letters from, Mrs Bentley?

MRS B: All sorts of people . . . ordinary people like ourselves . . .
film stars . . .

PROCTER: Film stars, Mrs Bentley? Which film stars?

MRS B: I can't remember.

PROCTER: Come on, love. Are they household names? Come on,
I'm sure my readers would be very interested.

MRS B: I'm sorry I don't remember.

PROCTER: Try love. Perhaps if I rattled off a few names some of them would click.

MRS B: There've been so many letters, so many phone calls . . .

(She breaks down.)

PROCTER: Alright, love. Clearly the nation is right behind you, Mrs Bentley. Could you tell me how you propose to harness this powerhouse of the public conscience?

MRS B: Pardon?

PROCTER: What are you going to do now?

MRS B: Oh I see . . . They think we should start a petition. Didn't seem much use before, but what else can we do now?

PROCTER: Who's organising the petition, Mrs Bentley?

MRS B: We've got a letter ready and all kinds of people have offered to help us get signatures for it.

PROCTER: So you could say the hopes of the Bentley household are pinned on the petition, eh Mrs Bentley?

MRS B: The law's said he should be hung. What else can we do?

PROCTER: Don't ask me, missus, how should I know?

(MRS BENTLEY goes.)

Scene Six

The PETITIONER enters, holding copies of the petition. She talks to the audience.

PETITIONER: I've got here a petition for the reprieve of Derek Bentley. I've got nearly 100,000 signatures and need more. Will you read the petition and if you agree with it, please sign.

(She hands them out to the audience, then sees PROCTER.)

PETITIONER: Will you sign this, sir?

PROCTER (looking at a copy): Petition for the reprieve of Derek Bentley. Very interesting. Having any success with it?

PETITIONER: Most people sign. I reckon we'll get over 100,000 signatures.

PROCTER: 100,000 eh? Not bad. (She continues with handing out.) Er excuse me — are all these people against hanging?

PETITIONER: No, not all.

PROCTER: Just against hanging Derek Bentley?

PETITIONER: That's right.

PROCTER: Just a moment. One more thing — when you get all these signatures you're going to take them to the Home Secretary I presume?

Example 115

PETITIONER: Yes, of course. He's the only one who can pardon Bentley now. Excuse me.

(The PASSER-BY enters.)

Excuse me, sir, will you sign the petition for the reprieve of Derek Bentley?

PASSER-BY: Sorry, no.

(He starts to move off.)

PROCTER: Could you tell me why you haven't signed the petition?

PASSER-BY: Who are you?

PROCTER (producing press card): Harry Procter, Sunday Pictorial.

PETITIONER (to PROCTOR): If you're not going to sign the petition can I have it back as there are people here who'll sign.

PROCTER: Look, love, I'm trying to conduct an interview here. Are you blind? (To PASSER-BY.) Sorry about that, sir. Now, could you tell me why you didn't sign the petition?

PASSER-BY: I think it's a lot of fuss over nothing. If everybody goes mad with petitions every time some young thug gets sentenced to death, how will our police be safe?

PROCTER: So you think it's not fair to the police?

Collecting signatures for petition to reprieve Derek.

PASSER-BY: Very strongly. Who's thinking about the poor widow of the policeman now? Who's making a fuss about here? £2.16 a week pension that's all she gets. That'd be worth getting up a petition about.

PETITIONER: I agree but –

PASSER-BY: But the real question is, can we really ask the police to risk their lives on our behalf if they don't feel they're supported by everybody and specially protected if things go wrong. That's the main point. How do you think they'll feel if this Bentley boy gets off?

PETITIONER: But –

PASSER-BY (to PETITIONER): I'm sorry but your petition's a complete waste of time.

(He goes.)

PETITIONER (calling after him): But Mrs Miles herself thinks Bentley should be reprieved.

PROCTER (to audience): Oh, yeah, did you hear about that? Touching little scene it was. Policeman's Widow Says Bentley Should Not Hang. I mean, not quite page one but pretty strong for page two.

PETITIONER: Look, are you going to sign or not?

PROCTER (handing it back): I don't think I'll bother. I mean the Press should remain impartial after all. And I mean, you've got more than enough signatures for the Home Secretary.

(The PETITIONER has collected in the petitions during this.)

PROCTER: Do you mind if I come along to take a picture of your handing in the petition?

PETITIONER: If you must.

(Slide of MAXWELL-FYFE, Home Secretary.)

NARRATOR: Sir David Maxwell-Fyfe, Home Secretary.

PETITIONER: We would like to present a petition on behalf of Derek William Bentley at present under sentence of death.

(A hand appears to receive the petition from her. PROCTER takes photo.)

SPOKESMAN (off): The Home Secretary will give your petition due consideration. The parents of the prisoner will be informed of his decision in due course.

(The PETITIONER tries to speak.)

That is all.

PROCTER: Thanks for the pic, mate. Don't reckon much to your chances though.

Example 117

PETITIONER: Oh really?

PROCTER: Yes, really. I mean Maxwell-Fyfe's not only the Home Secretary, but he's also the head of the Police Force and it was a policeman that got it wasn't it?

PETITIONER: Why don't you shut up, you parasite?

(She goes. PROCTOR laughs.)

PROCTER: Well, we'll wait and see, won't we.

(The slide of MAXWELL-FYFE stays. The sound of heartbeats is heard. PROCTER counts on his fingers, occasionally glancing at the slide of MAXWELL-FYFE.)

PROCTER: Fifteen days to go
fourteen days to go
thirteen days to go
twelve days to go
eleven days to go
ten days to go
nine days to go
eight days to go
seven days to go
six days to go
five days to go
four days to go
three days to go
two days to go . . .

Scene Seven

The slide and heartbeats fade. MRS BENTLEY enters. PROCTER crosses to her.

PROCTER: Mrs Bentley, Mrs Bentley, is it true the Home Secretary's rejected the petition?

MRS B: Rejected it?

PROCTER: You've heard nothing, Mrs Bentley?

MRS B: No, nothing. We're still waiting.

PROCTER: Oh.

MRS B: Why, what have you heard?

PROCTER: You've not had any word then?

MRS B: No messenger's been, nothing.

PROCTER: You've not had a letter, have you?

MRS B: Letter! . . . You'd better come in. The house is full of letters but surely . . .

Procter sorts through Mrs. Bentley's mail.

PROCTER: Perhaps you'd better take a look through them, Mrs Bentley.

MRS B: But surely . . .

PROCTER: An official-looking envelope, Mrs Bentley, are you sure you haven't seen one?

MRS B: But surely they wouldn't send it by ordinary post. They couldn't leave us waiting.

PROCTER: Take a look, Mrs Bentley.

(She brings out a large basket filled with letters. She empties it on the ground and starts searching through, eventually she finds the envelope. She opens it and starts to read.)

PROCTER: Is that it, Mrs Bentley? What does it say?

(She stays kneeling silent and broken.)

Look up, Mrs Bentley.

(She looks up. He takes a photo. PROCTER leaves. The heartbeats start up again. The mother stays on her knees.)

Example 119

Scene Eight

SILVERMAN (as he enters): Mrs Bentley, Mrs Bentley –

(Slide of SILVERMAN. He goes to MRS BENTLEY and during the following, helps her up.)

MRS B: What?

SILVERMAN: My name's Silverman. I'm an M.P. Some of us have heard about your son's case and want to do something about it.

MRS B: But the Home Secretary –

SILVERMAN: We're going to force a debate in the House of Commons tonight. There are important factors that weren't taken into account at the trial, factors such as your son's epilepsy and his low I.Q. He must be reprieved. Will you come?

(Pause.)

MRS B: Yes, of course.

(They cross the stage. Heartbeats again.)

Scene Nine

Sound of general hubbub. Slide: "The Commons Debate 27th January 1953, evening." SILVERMAN shows MRS BENTLEY to a seat.

SILVERMAN: Sit there, Mrs Bentley, in the public gallery.

SPEAKER (tape): Order! Order!

(Fade hubbub as SILVERMAN starts.)

SILVERMAN: Mr Speaker! Mr Speaker, yesterday shortly after 7.00 p.m. I presented for debate the motion "that this House does not agree with the Home Secretary's decision that there are not sufficient reasons for reprieving Derek Bentley, and urges him to reconsider the matter so far as to give effect to the recommendation of the jury and to the expressed view of the Lord Chief Justice that Bentley's guilt was less than that of his co-defendant, Christopher Craig." I have since been told by 'phone that on your instructions, the motion has been removed from the order paper. Is the House to wait until Bentley is dead before it is entitled to say he should not die?

SPEAKER (tape): In this case the motion of the honourable member which I saw last night dealt with the case of a capital sentence which is still pending and there is a long line of authorities of all my predecessors saying that, if a capital sentence is pending, the matter shall not be discussed by the House.

SILVERMAN: Mr Speaker, this is a matter which arouses interest of the deepest kind not merely in the House. I venture to think that if it were possible to put such a matter to the vote today, there would be an overwhelming majority of this House who think that the Home Secretary has decided wrongly. I have here more than 200 telegrams from all sorts of people all over the country, all of them except one holding the decision to be wrong, and that one telling me to mind my own business. Sir, I *am* minding my own business! That is why I am raising this question with you. It is the business of all of us if this boy is hanged when we think he ought not to be hanged. This is a parliamentary democracy and we are all responsible for what occurs.

SPEAKER (tape): A motion can be put down on this subject when the sentence has been executed, the Minister responsible may be criticised on the relevant vote of Supply or on the Adjournment. I have stated that this is the practice of the House and I cannot alter the practice of the House.

SILVERMAN: A three-quarter witted boy is to be hanged for a murder that he did not commit and which was committed fifteen minutes after he was arrested. Can we be made to keep silent when a thing as horrible and shocking as this is to happen?

SPEAKER (tape): I repeat that no debate on the subject can be held here until the execution has taken place. Only then can the justice of that execution be debated. That is my ruling based on all available Parliamentary precedent.

(Blank slide. Pause. SILVERMAN returns to where MRS BENTLEY sits silently.)

SILVERMAN: I'm sorry, Mrs Bentley.

MRS B: That's it then.

SILVERMAN: By no means, Mrs Bentley, don't give up now. A group of us are going to go to the Home Secretary's house tonight to argue with him face to face. We have signatures from 200 M.P.s. He must listen to us. (Pause.) I think you should go to your son, Mrs Bentley.

(Pause.)

MRS B: Yes.

SILVERMAN: We'll save him, Mrs Bentley. The Home Secretary will listen. Go and see Derek.

(Both leave. The heartbeats again. Silence.)

Scene Ten

Sound of crowd noises. PROCTOR dashes on and.goes to the phone.

PROCTER: The time 8.50 a.m. the 28th January, 1953, and only ten minutes to go before Derek Bentley is due to be executed. Outside Wandsworth Prison a large and angry crowd has gathered to protest. The chants of "Murder . . . murder" changed to cheers a few moments ago when a telegram boy arrived but it was a false

Example 121

alarm. He was not bringing Derek Bentley's reprieve. Even now extra squads of police are standing by in case the crowd breaks into the prison to try to save Bentley. With only minutes to go now, the crowd has grown strangely quiet but no-one is leaving. The life of Derek William Bentley now hangs on the thin thread of a last minute change of heart by the Home Secretary who appears to have ignored the deputation of M.P.s. Meanwhile, inside the prison, Derek William Bentley dictates his last letter . . .

(PROCTOR puts down the receiver and goes. Silence.)

Scene Eleven

BENTLEY enters.

BENTLEY: Dear Mum and Dad, I was so glad to see you on my visit today. I got the rosary and the letter and I saw the photo of the dog. Iris looked nice surrounded by all those animals. I could not keep the photo because it was a newspaper cutting. I told you, Mum, it would be very difficult to write this letter. I can't think of anything to say except you have all been wonderful the way you worked for me. Don't forget what I told you, "Always keep your chin up," and tell Pop not to grind his teeth. I hope Dad has more televisions in. Oh, I forgot to ask him how things were on the visit. Oh, Dad, don't let my cycle frames get rusty because they might come in handy one day and, Dad, keep a strict eye on Denis if he does anything wrong, though I don't think he will, but you never know how little things can get you into trouble. If he does, wallop him so that he won't sit down for three weeks. I am trying to give you good advice because of my experience. I tell you, Mum, the truth of this story has got to come out one day and as I said in the visiting box, one day a lot of people are going to get into trouble and I think you know who those people are. What do you think, Mum? This letter may sound a bit solemn but I am still keeping my chin up as I want all the family to do.

Don't let anything happen to the dogs and cats and look after them as you always have. I hope Laurie and Iris get married alright, I'd like to give them my blessing, it would be nice to have a brother-in-law like him. Laurie and I used to have some fun up at the pond till four o'clock in the morning, by the cafe. I always caught Laurie to pay for the pies, he never caught me. That will be all for now. I will sign this myself. Lots of love, Derek.

(The heartbeats start up. BENTLEY leaves. The heartbeats gradually fade. Pause. Enter NARRATOR.)

NARRATOR: Derek Bentley was hanged for the murder of P.C. Miles 28th January, 1953.

(She leaves.)

The End.

EXAMPLE - The Case of Craig and Bentley

Workshop Section

The workshop session lasted approximately two hours. It took place in the afternoon, after the performance. Sometimes the same space was used; sometimes the team moved round to another space in the school. One member of the team acted as Control Figure, and the others worked with the students in small groups. The pattern of the workshop was as follows:

1) Students arrive. As soon as they enter the space (which has been cleared of all furniture) they are encouraged to remove restrictive clothing and place their bags at the side of the room. The Control Figure introduces the team and gives a brief explantion of the pattern the workshop will follow. This moves quickly into:
2) Names - all students and actor-teachers try to introduce themselves and shake hands with everyone in the room in one minute.
3) Two more 'ice-breaker' games follow. The first of these is 'Keeper of the Keys', in which a set of keys has to be retrieved from under the chair of a blindfolded player without the thief being noticed or caught. The second game, 'Hunter and Hunted' involves two students at a time, both blindfolded, in the centre of a circle of students. One is the Hunter, and by careful listening he must attempt to catch the other, whose job is to keep out of the Hunter's clutches. Both games encourage silence, concentration and a certain amount of suspense, as well as relaxing the students.
4) Controller assigns groups of students to the other actor-teachers, who are positioned around the space.
5) In the groups the actor-teachers introduce themselves again and ask for students' names. In their groups they play two more 'ice-breaker' games.
   a) 'Killer' - one student is the detective and leaves the room, while the killer is chosen. By winking at students in the circle (or by any other agreed sign) the killer commits as many murders as possible without being detected by the detective who stands in the middle of the circle when the game begins.
   b) 'Detective' - the actor-teacher says 'Now I'm going to be a Detective and ask you all questions. I want you all to answer as one person, so if I ask you a question, Pauline, and then ask John the same question five minutes later, John must give the same reply. Got it? Right, what's your first name?' etc.
6) As the Controller begins to introduce the next item, an argument breaks out between two actor-teachers, rapidly developing into a fierce fight. Several of the other actor-teachers become involved in this fight, either verbally, physically, or both. At the end of the fight, one of the original fighters is 'dead'. The fight is very realistic, and can be repeated move for move and word for word by the actors. As the fight ends the Controller informs the students

Example 123

that it was not 'for real' (sometimes necessary), but that they are going to treat it as if it were. The students are informed that they must now work with their group leaders in preparing a statement detailing what they have just seen and heard. The students are told by the group leaders that they must say only what they are absolutely positive they saw or heard, not what they think happened. The statement must be taken seriously, as if they are giving evidence at a murder trial. The actor-teachers do not lead the questioning, ensuring that they only write down what the group tells them.

When the statements are completed, the Controller takes over again and reads them out. The actor-teachers act them as written while they are slowly read out. This is often hilarious, and unfailingly illustrates that statements are not as reliable as one imagines. Often the statements are a complete travesty of what actually took place. After each group's statement has been acted out, the actor-teachers repeat the real fight again, first slowly and then at the proper speed. The Controller concludes by pointing out that Derek Bentley was convicted largely on the basis of evidence given by witnesses operating in the dark, sometimes frightened, and with shots being fired at or by them. Some of the witnesses were out of sight of certain parts of the action which they heard. Nonetheless, Bentley was hanged. The major evidence which hangs him (that is the statement, 'Let him have it Chris') is always in dispute, Craig and Bentley claiming it was never spoken at all.

7) Next the Controller divides the students into pairs. The pairs are asked to label themselves 'a' and 'b'. A's go to one end of the room, and 'b's to other. At each end is an actor-teacher. Group 'a' are told that they are going to take part in an exercise with their partner, who will be playing their mother or father. The parent has found a knife in 'a's bedroom and wants an explanation of what it is for and where it came from. The 'a's are told that the knife has been forced on them for safe-keeping by a gang of youths with whom they are involved. This gang has threatened the 'a's with violent consequences if anything happens to the knife, or if the 'a's reveal where they got it from.

Meanwhile, the 'b's are told that as parents of 'a's, they are worried about the company their child is keeping and, having found a knife in their child's bedroom, must seek to discover where it came from and what it is for. The Controller waits until the relevant information has been transmitted to the 'a's and 'b's and then brings them quickly together. The improvisations take place simultaneously. If any of the pairs are having difficulty, the actor-teachers encourage them to continue and attempt to reach a conclusion. After approximately five minutes, the Controller stops the improvisations, informs the 'a's and 'b's what the other was told, and sets up discussion centring on the parents' responsibility and the child's allegiance to the group.

8) Next, the students are divided into three groups, labelled 'a', 'b' and 'c'. The 'a's are informed by an actor-teacher that they are magistrates trying the case of two youths already on probation, who are accused

of stealing a purse. They are informed that they must decide who is responsible and pass sentence. The 'b's are told that they are responsible for the purse theft. Being on probation, they wish to avoid any further conviction, and so must attempt to pass the blame on to 'c', who, they are told, is a bit stupid. The 'c's are told that they had no part in the theft and even though jointly accused, will not inform on their friend. This improvisation continues for approximately seven to eight minutes and concludes with a discussion, led by the Controller, which seeks to discover the motives of the magistrates in passing sentence, and the reaction of the accused to the events which unfold as the magistrate questions them.

9) Finally, the Controller leads a discussion with the whole group. The actor-teachers join in on specific points or questions as directed by the Controller. The aim is to discuss the issues raised by the programme, and answer any questions relating to the facts of the Craig and Bentley case. The students are encouraged to bear in mind the complexity of the examination of legal issues, and to remember their own confusions and problems in sorting out fact from fiction both as spectators and as participants.

NOTE: When the Bolton Octagon Theatre in Education Company (now known as M6 Theatre Company) performed this programme, they handled the Workshop session rather differently:

The students played two 'ice-breaker' games - Killer and Detective. Then the actor-teachers performed the fight, exactly as in (6) in the Coventry Workshop. Next, the students, in groups, questioned four characters from the play, still in role - Defence Council, Prosecution Council, Bentley's mother and Police Sergeant Fairfax. Each character moved to a new group after five minutes of questioning. Students were told that they were questioning these characters as a preliminary to a formal questioning session with Lord Chief Justice Goddard. They were asked to note any questions they wanted to ask him as a result of their questioning of the other four characters.

Lord Goddard arrives. He enters formally and sits on a rostrum. The Controller ensures that Lord Goddard does not make unfair statements unchallenged. Finally, there is a question and answer session with all the actor-teachers out of role on any points raised in the programme which the students want to discuss.

HOLLAND NEW TOWN

A one and a half day Theatre in Education project

Devised by the Bolton Octagon Theatre in Education Company*

CARETAKER (Mr Kay)   Mike Kay or Clive Russell
SOCIAL WORKER (Miss Williams) Cora Williams
CONTRACTOR (Mr Hargreaves)   Dave Swapp
TOWN PLANNER (Mrs Slade)   Yvette Vansen
COUNCILLOR (Mrs Kenning)   Eileen Kenning

Scenario by Cora Williams, Pam Schweitzer and Dave Swapp

*This company has subsequently become the M6 Theatre Company

Introduction to Holland New Town

Throughout the devising and playing of Holland New Town, the needs of the pupils came first. In other words, it was child-centred rather than subject-centred. In this case the 'child' was a group of not more than eighteen sixteen-year-olds. The time was 1973 and the pupils were the first ROSLA pupils (R.O.S.L.A. Raising of the School Leaving Age).

For some time prior to the Autumn of 1973 the Theatre-in-Education Company at the Octgon Theatre in its ongoing discussion with Bolton teachers, were aware of their fears and hopes for this extra year's education. At that time some teachers viewed the scheme as another chance for pupils to gain the proper qualifications they would need to compete in the job market. Other teachers were more apprehensive, especially for the less able pupils whose problems would never be solved within the examination system. It was for these pupils that *Holland New Town* was designed; for the brash and gauche, the rowdy and shy, the naive, lethargic and very vulnerable, in fact for those at the butt end of our education system. The schools planned to relax the secondary schools norms, classrooms would be less formal, time-tables reshaped to allow longer blocks of time, and fewer teachers would spend more time with their pupils. In other words, the ROSLA year was to resemble in many ways the primary school structure. More emphasis was to be placed on a study of the community in which the school was based with greater flexibility for out of school visits. However, it would still be school and it would still be very difficult to create enthusiasm for anything (including a T.I.E. programme) to do with school.

For all these reasons *Holland New Town* was a new departure in Theatre-in-Education. The programme would take place, not in schools, but in the Company's Studio, which would be turned over completely to the programme. Name plates and notices were removed, actors' personal belongings were locked away and telephones were altered to handle only calls written into the programme. The biggest change of all was the duration of the programme; it would run for one and a half days (apparently an extravagant use of time for just eighteen pupils, but a factor that proved crucial to the pupils' involvement). The structure was repetitive; formal talk, followed by semi-formal group-work, then informal tea-break, and back to formal talk and so on, each block of time requiring short concentration periods. The familiar structure gave the pupils security. It was even planned that they should be bored at times and deliberately distracted to overhear 'private' telephone calls and staffroom rows. They were apparently attending a course on town planning, but they became much more interested in the real-life drama of personalities and subsequently the corrupt scheme to defraud. As their lethargy gave way to curiosity the experienced T.I.E. actors fostered and controlled a potentially explosive situation. The sixteen-year-olds expect fairness and honesty from people in authority and they find themselves questioning technical expertise and local government infallibility and bureaucracy. They share between them the knowledge to expose the whole plot and by the end of one and a half days and often sooner, they can remain passive no longer.

At the end of the first performance the Company was faced with an unforseen problem. The pupils had gradually become so absorbed by the events that they believed the Town Planning Course and the corruption tale to be absolutely real. It left the teacher with an awkward situation, maybe restraining pupils from reporting the story to the police or the local paper. If they were left to discover the fictitious nature of the events for themselves they might feel 'conned' and dismiss the important learning experience together with their hurt feelings. Therefore, subsequent performances ended with a chat with the teacher (who had experienced the whole show) and the sympathetic characters. If necessary the fiction was explained and parallels were drawn with current corruption cases described in the news media.

If you are thinking of performing *Holland New Town*, please note that it is desirable that at least three of the five actors are experienced T.I.E. performers. In the fluid relationship between actors and pupils, the actors need an instinct for the drama in every situation and they must guard carefully the periods of theatre when everyone's attention can be arrested and refocussed on the pre-determined plot.

Cora Williams

SOURCES: The Company sought advice from the local planning department, who proved most helpful and interested. The programme coincided with a town planning exhibition in Bolton and several pupils visited this in the course of their one and a half day programme. The Poulson affair was raging during the devising period, which of course affected the Company's thinking on the plot, and press coverage of this issue was a primary source.

First performed in Bolton with the following actors: Michael Kay, Eileen Kenning, David Swapp, Yvette Vanson, Cora Williams.

Thirty pupils are told that they are going on a Town Planning Course for one and a half days. They arrive at the back entrance to the theatre, and queue up by a sign attached to the studio door saying 'Town Planning Course.'

First Day
1.45-2.00pm

Pupils	Caretaker (Mr Kay)	Social Worker (Miss Williams)	Contractor (Mr Hargreaves)	Town Planner (Mrs Slade)
Have to wait outside as door is not opened to their knocking.	Inside studio. It is his lunch-break, so he is refusing to open door before time.	Arrives early and, like pupils has to wait outside. Decides to do some shopping. 'Tell Mrs Slade I'll not be late' — to small group of pupils.	Arrives just before 2pm. Makes little effort to be friendly with the pupils. He is missing a business lunch for this and is not taking the course very seriously.	Arrives at 2pm and calls authoritatively to Caretaker to open door before time, which he does.
Once inside they are seated formally on benches facing a dais with four seats on. Formality of seating arrangement helps overcome pupils embarrassment at strangeness of place, and any possible boisterousness from having been kept waiting. They watch adults' reactions with interest.	Opens up when shouted at by Town Planner. Reluctantly follows her orders when she comes in. Is asked to move a case of bottles (present from Hargreaves) off her table into staffroom.	In fact she is late back and incurs Mrs Slade's displeasure!	It is understood that case of bottles on Slade's table is present from him.	Once inside she throws her weight around ordering Caretaker to re-arrange seating etc. She is friendly towards Hargreaves and acknowledges present from him of box of bottles.

Pupils gather for the Town Planning Course.

The social worker's group consider the problems involved in rehousing.

The studio is partitioned, so that there are several inter-connecting rooms. There is one central area with benches facing a dais and this is where the formal lectures take place. There is a staffroom with a telephone in it. This doubles as Mrs Slade's office. There is a game called Suburbia (see illustration) laid out in another room. The contractor's area contains estate agent's literature and some building plans. There is a room for the social worker with photographs of residents and some street plans up on the walls. In the Central Area where the pupils sit initially, there are 3-dimensional plans, architects drawings and public notices.

2.05-2.40pm

Pupils	Caretaker	Social Worker	Contractor	Town Planner
Pupils' attention is divided. They listen to the 'experts', but also register the caretaker's attitude, the rebuke for Miss Williams by Mrs Slade, the amicable relationship between Slade, the gift of the bottles, the fact that Mrs Slade is very much in charge, and the caretaker is very much the underdog.	Hovers throughout this session. Telephone rings and caretaker asks Mrs Slade to take the call. She is not pleased to be disturbed and tells him to take a message to get caller to ring back. Caretaker generally makes his somewhat reluctant presence felt during this session with noises off, sweeping, etc.	Knocks to be admitted. Apologises for lateness to Mrs Slade and everyone else. She speaks after contractor. She is a somewhat 'woolly' personality, but seems genuinely concerned about her cases. She raises questions of suitable housing for the old, for unmarried mothers, etc. She is clearly worried by some of the new housing policy.	Hargreaves is very much the man of the world, concerned with getting the job done, keeping afloat etc. His attitude towards women is chauvinistic, but he is jokey in a man-to-man style with the boys. He talks about how to get work from the council. He must tender for a job with other firms, so relies on past experience in quoting for a job,	Mrs Slade opens the course. It will give them a chance to hear experts speaking about their work in the local area. She announces that there will be lectures and group work. She introduces the contractor and announces (crossly) that Miss Williams is expected shortly. Goes to admit Miss Williams who arrives late and needs

Siting houses on the plan.

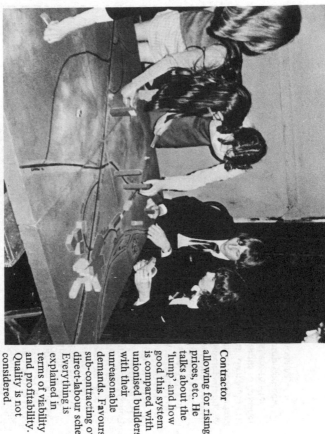

Contractor

allowing for rising prices, etc. He talks about the 'lump' and how good this system is compared with unionised builders with their unreasonable demands. Favours sub-contracting over direct-labour scheme. Everything is explained in terms of viability and profitability. Quality is not considered.

Town Planner

to be let in. She rebukes her and then they both take places on dais. After contractor has finished she introduces Miss Williams to the pupils. Her tone is very slightly disparaging, enough for the pupils to realise there is no great sympathy there.

Mrs Slade divides the pupils into three equal groups, A, B and C, and explains that these groups will rotate, so that each one works with each expert during the course. The pupils then go off into small rooms with a character, as instructed.

2.40-3.00pm

Pupils	Caretaker	Social Worker	Contractor	Town Planner
In small groups, the pupils had opportunity to (a) work hard on given assignment, (b) to chat alone in order to share reactions towards the characters and crystallise their feelings, especially towards Slade, (c) in one's and two's to wander with messages to other adults about equipment, temperature, etc. They had to locate caretaker for this and he wandered all the time, so there was of necessity some	In and out of his store-room. Pupils look on him for pencils, chairs, etc. He discreetly encourages exchanges of confidence about the course and personalities. He prepares for the tea-break, establishing number of cups needed with/ without sugar, etc., and some times interrupting groups.	*Group A* – They are asked to match price tags with different houses, to be demolished under slum clearance programme. Each house has a history. Many now empty. Talk of problems raised for particular families in street. Compensation they will receive will not buy substitute house of any kind. Reference made to badly built council housing, especially high rise blocks which are not attractive to Snipe Street residents and will be slums of the future.	*Group B* – Pupils explains the game *Suburbia* which is a 3-dimensional board on which certain housing and amenity blocks have to be sited. It is clear that Suburbia is a hypothetical town but is relevant to their study of Holland New Town. The game is simple and engrossing enough for Mrs Slade to leave her group on its own a lot while she circulates and telephones from her office. She calls on Miss Williams' group and quizzes them somewhat cynically in Miss Williams' short absence about the	*Group C* – Mrs Slade introduces concepts of leasehold, of style of house and position in town as determinant of value. Talks of cheaper ways of building now being developed. Shows model of one area of town and asks pupils to consider where to site proposed new housing,

Pupils	Caretaker	Social Worker	Contractor	Town Planner
awareness of what other groups were doing.			problems of subsidence, damp ground, pollution, noise, etc. He has definite preference for for building highrise council flats, as they 'don't need to be saleable anyway'. But housing with a careful eye to desirability and style.	Snipe Street case study and what they have been talking about.

3.00-3.10pm

TEA-BREAK — Tea is served by the caretaker in the Central area, and on tray, taken by two pupils, to adults in staffroom, where pupils notice that case of bottles, registered at the beginning on Slade's table, contains champagne which Mrs Slade is delighted with. Miss Williams spends most of tea break with pupils and caretaker where she feels more at ease than in staffroom. This was the pupils' first opportunity to talk with their teacher about the course. The best attitude for the teacher to adopt was that of loyal colleague of the 'professionals' — blinkered and insensitive to nuances of interest to pupils and not interested in hearing about the champagne, etc. Attitudes to smoking are related to character. There are 'no smoking' signs up, which Mrs Slade ignores, but she disapproves of pupils smoking. Caretaker smokes in his own room. If asked by pupils for permission to smoke, Hargreaves says he couldn't care less whether they do or not. Miss Williams says 'I don't know what to say you'd better ask Mrs Slade.' Result: — some pupils, usually boys, smoked daringly in caretaker's room, and in return for his tolerance, identified with him and built up sympathy with him in his job.

Two more fifteen-minute group sessions, co-ordinated by Mrs Slade, giving each group the opportunity to try the exercises previously described.

Pupils

Throughout these sessions pupils are increasingly aware of different attitudes amongst the adults. Word is passing around about the champagne and the Slade phone calls. Disagreements between Miss Williams and Mr Hargreaves are registered and informally passed around in discussion. There is plenty of time for the pupils to chat when they are left by their 'tutor' to get on with the work.

Caretaker

Answers telephone twice. (1) Call from Town Hall and he has to explain that it is needed for a town planning course. Asked to explain it to the caller, he is clearly a bit non-plussed by the whole course. (2) Call from Mr Slade to ask his wife to bring the plans home. She leaves group to take call, and chats to them, asks them what they are doing in suburbia

Social Worker   Contractor

There is interchange between these two groups over the heating (Miss Williams' room is underheated and caretaker points out that heat is controlled from Hargreaves' room) and then over the question of house prices. Miss Williams' group want to know why houses being built now are so expensive and why can't cheaper houses be made. Hargreaves explains about raising capital, paying back interest, soaring building costs, material costs rising, etc. It is made clear that Miss Williams is unhappy about wholesale demolition of areas like Snipe Street, whereas Hargreaves likes neat solutions. He reckons rehabilitation of Snipe Street a non-starter, throwing good money after bad, etc. Pupils observe different reactions of these characters and have opportunity to talk about them during these sessions.

Town Planner

Caretaker calls her to the phone. She leaves group but is audible to at least some of the pupils while she speaks on the office phone to her husband. She says she will be late home because of difficulty over the contract, but she'll bring the plans with her and is sure it will all go through, etc. This is a first scent of the sub-plot for the pupils who usually share the information with the rest of the group in Slade's absence. If they do not listen to her Slade can tell them to be quiet as

Mrs. Slade gives a formal talk on town planning.

Informality is the keynote with Mrs. Williams, the social worker.

Pupils	Caretaker	Social Worker	Contractor	Town Planner
	game, etc. Why are they giving all best sites for private housing instead of council, etc. They patiently explain that if they don't the private houses won't sell. He is not at all happy with this idea and says they should be prepared to try something new.			she can't hear on the telephone.

3.40-3.55pm

Final lecture of the first day in Central area. Pupils assemble in rows. Course leaders take places on dais in front.

3.40-3.55

Pupils	Caretaker	Social Worker	Contractor	Town Planner
Pupils attention is divided between the talks and the 'goings-on with the telephone, slide projector arguments	Sets up slide projector to illustrate Slade's talk. Phone rings and he announces call for Mrs Slade	She is barely able to refrain her anger at the contractor's attitude in his talk. She talks about the social dangers of	Talks about necessary profit margin for healthy industry, healthy competition in the building trade, the need to attract	Mrs Slade introduces the final session of the day and asks Mr Hargreaves to speak first. She is called to the phone by the

Pupils	Caretaker	Social Worker	Contractor	Town Planner
between characters, treatment of caretaker etc.	from A and B Contractors. When caretaker operates slide projector he is criticised sarcastically when he makes mistakes, eg. slide up-side down or sideways. He shows increasing interest as Mrs Slade talks and follows her finger on the plan very carefully. Caretaker enlists pupils help in clearing up.	high rise living and the health hazards in existing poor housing. Feels people should come before profit, and urgent ways should be explored for improving existing housing and preserving communities.	investors by demonstrating profitability, etc. Sees the whole question of housing in financial terms, as opposed to Miss Williams' humanistic approach. He is clearly very put out that A and B Contractors are in touch with Slade.	caretaker to speak to A and B Contractors. Mrs Slade clearly thinks Miss Williams' outburst is absurd and she cuts her short 'in view of the time'. She talks (illustrated with slides) about redevelopment in Holland New Town, and replacement of 'eye-sores' with new homes and roads. She refers pupils to model in the Central area and points out housing area which should be cleared. She concludes day and tells pupils to be there at 10 am prompt the following day.

Pupils stay to help caretaker to clear up. He refers them to the model and shows them where he lives, in the 'eye-sore' bit. He promises to show them some pictures of his house if they come early the following day. They agree to come early. They leave.

Three speakers leave, Miss Williams alone, and Mrs Slade accepting a lift from Mr Hargreaves, within pupils' hearing.

At the end of the first day, the pupils have (a) a feeling of security with the formality of the structured sessions (like school) and (b) a curiosity about the adult relationships and (c) clues, in the form of snippets of over-heard conversation and observed reactions, which they will enjoy recalling the following day when they get deeper into the plot, and (d) a bond with the caretaker, identified as underdog, and demonstrating similar relationship with Slade to that of ROSLA pupil with teachers.

Second Day
9.30-10.00pm

Pupils

The pupils arrive at 9.30 (or even earlier) to meet the caretaker as arranged the previous day. They come in informal groups of twos and threes. The caretaker shows them his snapshots of home and family. He wants them to see the changes he has made to improve his house, adding a bathroom and redecorating, etc. It is a modest, but now structurally sound terraced house. Late-comers are 'filled in' by friends who have heard the whole story and who borrow caretaker's photos to illustrate. Caretaker's house is again located on the Holland New Town model so the pupils understand that planning decisions affect real people and the homes they have a pride in.

Caretaker Social Worker Contractor Town Planner

These three arrive at 10 am separately, but in quick succession and the atmosphere is abruptly changed. There is an instinctive movement to hide the photos from Mrs Slade, but often, later in the day, pupils will ask the caretaker if he/she can borrow them to show Miss Williams as they connect with the things she discusses. Mrs Slade brings with her Councillor Kenning, a Labour Councillor. She has a frumpish hat and generally more homely appearance than the chic Mrs Slade, but is not as informal and relaxed with the pupils as Miss Williams. She is self-educated and has local accent.

10.00-10.20am

The pupils assemble for the first lecture. For the rest of the morning the caretaker is in the background, but he has contact with the pupils during the tea-break, and sometimes is able to push the plot along by asking the right questions.

Pupils	Social Worker	Contractor	Town Planner	Councillor Kenning
Pupils sit on benches arranged formally as on the first day. Pupils are a little surprised at intensity of feeling aroused by the apparently mild and bland Councillor Kenning in Miss Williams. However, they now know Miss Williams enough to trust her judgement, and become rather suspicious of the Councillor.	When Councillor says how important it is to keep politics out of local government, Miss Williams is furious. She argues that Councillors are elected by local people because they have particular policies which are tied in with their political ideas. Their job is to put these policies into operation. She clearly feels Councillor Kenning is ineffective as a local representative and is out of touch		Introduces Mrs Kenning, a Labour Councillor who is interested in education and is a member of the housing committee and the transport committee. Mrs Slade joins in at the last point made by Councillor Kenning to demonstrate two alternative routes for the flyover. She uses a plastic flyover on the 3-dimensional model showing it either going over the caretaker's house or over some large	She introduces the idea of being a councillor and explains how she became involved, itemising acts of philanthropy which have brought her to public office. She talks about ruling labour group policy – major redevelopment and demolition of slum areas in Holland New Town and their replacement with modern council flats. Her own pet interests are housing and transport. She refers to an important meeting she must attend that afternoon to determine

Pupils	Social Worker	Contractor	Town Planner	Councillor Kenning
	with real people and their problems.		houses which have been converted into flats.	siting of new major road and flyover through Holland New Town.

10.20am

Pupils	Caretaker	Social Worker	Contractor	Town Planner	Cllr. Kenning
Pupils are now divided into their three groups and they visit each of the experts in turn, with the exception of Mrs Slade who spends most of her time on the staffroom telephone frequently audible. The pupils are now more confident about leaving their group on a	More in evidence now preparing next tea-break. He calls on group working with Cllr. Kenning, in her absence, to collect tea orders and has portable tape recorder with him. Records them unawares and plays it back for everyone to have a laugh. Leaves it running and there is Slade's voice. She is	In room near staffroom where Slade can be heard. Pupils are asked to look at some case studies of (a) unmarried mother turned out of her home, (b) newly widowed grandmother who wants to move into house with daughter's family, etc. Pupils work in pairs to discuss possible solutions	Group looks at different ways of building, comparing speed and durability. Hargreaves gives them (in twos) (a) paper + blue tack – to simulate pre-stressed concrete, (b) pre-cut card + blue tack in + blue walls with door + window holes already cut – to simulate prefabricated dwellings and	Slade moves from group to group and talks on telephone to husband, solicitor and A + B Contractors. Within pupils' hearing she and Hargreaves have battle over the road-building contract and why she is in touch with A + B Contractors. He is clearly afraid she is	Group become councillors working through a typical agenda, which Cllr. Kenning finds in her bag. She explains it to them and asks them to debate and take decisions on the following: (a) whether the local museum should charge entry fee, (b) whether a highly contested

Pupils	Caretaker	Social Worker	Contractor	Town Planner	Cllr. Kenning
pretext, eg. lavatory, if they want to communicate with other pupils or the caretaker.	talking to her solicitor about buying cheaply some big houses which are threatened by the new road, whose position is not yet certain. Caretaker and pupils very suspicious now.	to these problems which all relate to housing difficulties. Pupils discuss relative merits. Miss Williams suggests they question Cllr. Kenning on these when they have a session with her. Slade visits the group and embarasses Miss Williams. When she goes, Slade leaves behind a contract by mistake. Pupils discover it and realise that Slade's husband is buying up the big houses by the proposed flyover which were	(c) *Lego* bricks to build wall. Pupils discuss about tendering for corporation work including road building. Explains that it usually goes to the lowest bidder but if you undercut too much you lose your profit and reputation. Gives pupils to understand that inside information can come in very handy here, 'a nod is as good as a wink,' etc.	tricking him, but she is suave and dismissive about the whole thing. She is consistently charming towards Councillor Kenning, and has quiet words with her about current council matters, especially the cleaner who has contracted dermatitis at work. When Cllr. leaves group, Caretaker calls on them with tape recorder (see his column.) Slade is very charming towards Cllr., and they talk privately about	fish and chip shop should be built bearing in mind the strength of public opinion for and against, and (c) how much compensation should be paid to a council cleaner who has contracted

Pupils	Caretaker	Social Worker	Contractor	Town Planner	Cllr. Kenning
		threatened with demolition before new alternative route was proposed. Pupils locate these houses on the model.			the forthcoming council meeting. When she leaves, Cllr. turns to pupils and explains that she takes advice from such experts as Mrs Slade.

10.40am

Tea-break, during which Mrs Slade answers telephone near to pupils' tea trolley. If they are not listening in to her call (they usually are) she asks them to be quiet so she can hear properly. There is a call from her husband about the houses. She refers to plan A and plan B, and says that Cllr. Kenning is amenable. Then she and Kenning and Hargreaves retire rather furtively, for some urgent talk about tenders and contracts. Pupils who have seen Mrs Slade's contract for the house in Miss Williams' room, call friends from other groups to see it secretly.

10.55-11.40am

Pupils	Caretaker	Social Worker	Contractor	Town Planner	Cllr. Kenning
In rotating groups so that each samples the work described for the	Makes many informal references back to his home and the photos. He makes greater use	Miss Williams' group uses the Slade housing contract and come to	Two more groups try his building experiment. He clearly favours the reinforced concrete	Still visiting the different groups, ostensibly to see that all is going well. But the	Repeats of Agenda session, but also goes round to other groups and

Pupils	Caretaker	Social Worker	Contractor	Town Planner	Cllr. Kenning
10.20-10.40 session. Two of these group sessions take the pupils up to the final morning lecture. There is quite a lot of to-ing and fro-ing between groups in these sessions.	of the model towards the climax, pointing out his house and how it is threatened by Plan B, the new plan devised by Slade to be put to Council that afternoon.	understand how it would be in her interest for plan B for the new road to be adopted. They replace document in or near Slade's case before it is missed.	method for cheapness. Explains how labour-intensive, and therefore problematical brickwork is. He is clearly fairly on edge in his dealings with Slade and Cllr. Kenning in these sessions.	pupils sense that she is spying on Miss Williams whom she regards as incompetent, placating the angry Hargreaves, and buttering up Cllr. Kenning.	expresses interest in what they are doing. She says how important she thinks this town planning course is for the pupils.

11.40-12.00 am

Final lecture of the morning. Pupils assemble on benches in central area. Mr Hargreaves and Miss Williams simply observe this session.

Pupils	Caretaker	Town Planner	Councillor Kenning
Pupils are by now very alert to the implications for the caretaker of the proposed new road, as the bright orange plastic strip gets moved back and forth to illustrate	He is operating projector and puts up other visual aids – draft plans, etc. for Cllr. Kenning and Mrs Slade. He listens and watches very carefully now, to see how plans affect his home. He	Mrs Slade introduces Cllr. Kenning's final session by explaining that there are two possible routes (Plans A + B) for the new ring road and flyover. She	Explanation offered of how residents affected by road building are compensated in proportion to the value of their house. Pupils often question (recalling their session with Miss Williams the

Pupils	Caretaker	Town Planner	Councillor Kenning
Plans A and B. The pupils watch the caretaker and want to exchange glances with him. They hover round at the end of the session to talk to him, but they are frustrated by Slade.	does not display emotion, but the pupils know he is really concerned.	explains that its sitting will have implications for the owners of the properties that lie in its path. She moves the proposed road (bright orange plastic) menacingly about the board to demonstrate its effect in Plans A + B. Slade clears pupils out at lunch-time, as otherwise the actor playing the caretaker would get no lunch-break.	previous day) why compensation is rarely sufficient to buy an equivalent house. Cllr. points out that building costs on new roads and new housing are sky-high and the council cannot afford sufficient compensation when contractors like Mr Hargreaves put in such high tenders, etc. She has to hurry off to the meeting where the road will be discussed. Slade hastily checks that Cllr. has both plans with her. She asks pupils if they would like her to call in after the meeting to tell them what has been decided. They always say yes.

2pm

Pupils usually come back early and the caretaker lets them in. They chat, not usually offering specific help, but offering physical solidarity and sharing his anxiety by hovering sympathetically. Sometimes pupils wander into the staffroom and light upon air-line tickets for the 'Slades – a present from A + B Contractors, or upon the champagne. Caretaker is meanwhile preparing the room for a planned lecture. The three speakers arrive, and Mrs Slade is clearly anxious, frequently checking the time, sending pupils to answer imaginary knocks at the door, etc. She says there is no time for a lecture now and instead divides pupils into their groups again.

2.10pm

Pupils	Caretaker	Social Worker	Contractor	Town Planner
Pupils are on edge, and Mrs Slade's mood kindles a restlessness, bordering on ill-discipline which is necessary to give them the nerve to discover the plot for themselves. Some seek teacher's approval for their detective work, feeling guilty about it if they still see the whole event as real. If they think it is a fiction they are bolder in chasing the clues.	The one person who does not leave the building in this session. He leads from behind the discovery of the connections between different 'clues'. He alerts them to phone calls, documents, bottles and air-line tickets, on the rare occasions they do not spot these for themselves. But his attitude is cynical rather than excitement about discoveries.	Discusses how, with Council grants a family can improve their home as a viable alternative to re-housing in council flats. A show-case near Town Hall provides excuse to go out and all necessary visual aids for the session. In shadow of Town Hall the plausibility of the whole 'course' was enhanced. Miss Williams is horrified by discoveries about Slade, but doesn't condone pupils' searching her belongings, etc.	He settles his group to look at a 3-dimensional plan of proposed suburb of Holland New Town, and consider suitable housing sites. Then he goes off to search for Slade when she leaves the building. This group overhear phone call between Slade and her solicitor about 'hurrying the deal through'. Some of them decide to follow Hargreaves into town and see what he does.	Mrs Slade asks her group to site amenity blocks on the suburbia board and she rushes off into town. If asked why, she says she's going to buy evening paper for council meeting coverage. She leaves brief-case open in staffroom containing contracts for large houses under route A and air-line tickets to Bahamas — gift from A + B Builders. The pupils left on their own explore the staffroom and find these. Some follow her into town to see what she does.

Pupils	Caretaker	Social Worker	Contractor	Town Planner
		She is very confused about what to do.		

2.15-2.45pm

Planner and Contractor and Some Pupils

In the town there are pupils from all three groups. Some will be with Miss Williams looking at the Bolton Planning Department Exhibition. Some are 'tracking' Hargreaves and some 'tracking' Slade. These two, approaching from different directions, meet at the pre-arranged post where pupils could listen to them without being seen. There is argument. Hargreaves claims he has been deceived by Slade. She advised him to tender for Holland New Town Ring Road at £Xm and he suspects she's also been negotiating with another builder. He heard her disuading Cllr. Kenning from supporting the Hargreaves bid. Mrs Slade denies it all and goes back to the course.

Pupils

The pupils are now tending to move around in twos and threes with the exception of Miss Williams' group, most of whom stay together to go to the exhibition. These small groups of pupils do one of the following:-

(a) stay in the group's room and carry on working
(b) go and talk with the caretaker
(c) waste time
(d) rediscover champagne
(e) discover plane tickets to Bahamas from A + B Contractors
(f) listen to tape recordings
(g) discover documents
(h) follow Mr Hargreaves or Mrs Slade into town and 'track' their movements.
(i) do a lot of cross-reporting —i.e. group too timid to explore staffroom would receive fact and opinion from those who did. These verbal exchanges were important to make sure all followed the plot.

2.45-3.15pm

Tea-break with everyone back in the building. Then Mrs Slade asserts her authority and orders a quiet hard-working session in their groups. All groups change around and work with a different character. In terms of the drama of the situation this 'hard-working' session creates greater secrecy and tension — much whispering and furtive movement. Pupils turn more often to the Caretaker and Miss Williams for leadership and for a spokesperson who can stand up to Mrs Slade as they feel the situation is getting beyond them. The Caretaker will not take any initiative however. Little work is done by the pupils on their ostensible tasks, but most of them go through the motions of working.

3.15pm

Pupils are assembled in central area for final lecture. Cllr. Kenning has empty chair placed waiting for her. Session starts without her.

Pupils	Caretaker	Social Worker	Contractor	Town Planner	Councillor
Tremendous air of excitement among the pupils at this point.	Stands by with model and ringroad piece.	Sits at the back with the pupils.	Makes feeble excuse, grabs coat and says he has to go out but will be back shortly.	Starts to talk about professionals like her in local government and their relationship with lay councillors like Kenning. Her mind is clearly on other things during this talk and she looks at her watch a lot,	Councillor breezes in at 3.20 from council meeting. She and Mrs Slade speak privately and secret. Slade is clearly delighted. They announce that pupils will now be let into the secret. Slade recaps plans

Pupils	Caretaker	Social Worker	Contractor	Town Planner	Councillor
Pupils keep anxious check on Caretaker to see how he takes the news. The effect of seeing the little wooden blocks on the floor is traumatic for him and the pupils. Pupils are astounded by Hargreave's outburst, they remain very still and alert to the end of the session. There is a sense of	When Slade and Hargreaves leave, Caretaker accuses Cllr. of irresponsibility. He explains about his house and the improvements he's made. She says he will get compensation, and is sorry but it is all in the name of progress, and small sacrifices must be made. When Cllr. leaves he	She is embarrassed and horrified by the revelations of the afternoon, but she does not want to capitalise/ sensationalise them like Hargreaves does. She is sympathetic towards Caretaker, but paralysed.	Hargreaves comes back in just before final decision is made. From back of central area Hargreaves (unnoticed till this point) asks who got the contract for building the new ring road. When Cllr. replies that A + B builders did he turns angrily on planner and lets rip about local government corruption and how she has abused her	sends pupils to door. etc. Big build up with model to 'And now Cllr. will you tell us which have agreed to?' When she hears the answer she sweeps the little wooden blocks, representing 'slums', including Caretaker's house, to the floor. The orange plastic road is removed from 'posh' houses and placed over where Caretaker's house stood. Pupils see that Mrs Slade's newly	A + B: A over posh houses (now owned by Slade as pupils know) and B over 'slums' (where caretaker's nice little house is as pupils know.) Cllr. cheerfully announces that Plan B has been accepted, the better solution she now thinks. She is slightly embarrassed at having to tell the contractor that A + B contractors got the road contract. She says she hopes

Pupils	Caretaker	Social Worker	Contractor	Town Planner	Councillor
disappointment at the discovery that there is little that the Caretaker or Miss Williams can do about the situation.	turns to Miss Williams who reminds him that he can object to the plan and get the questions re-opened, but he does not believe that anyone with influence will support him, when people like A + B Contractors and Slade and Kenning want the scheme to go ahead and have money invested in it.	she can but is clearly not very confident that he can get the decision reversed. She is most unhappy about the new plan and the way in which the decision was made.	position and he is going to the press about it (now he no longer stands to benefit by it.) He makes for the door. He maintains council took decision on her advice.	acquired houses, bought so cheaply are now worth a fortune as no longer threatened. Slade tries to stop Hargreaves saying it was not her decision. It rested with the council. She apologises to Cllr. Kenning.	it has been interesting for them to see how local government works and how interesting it can be. 'Work will soon start on the new road.'

They both leave studio arguing furiously and he threatening to go to the press.

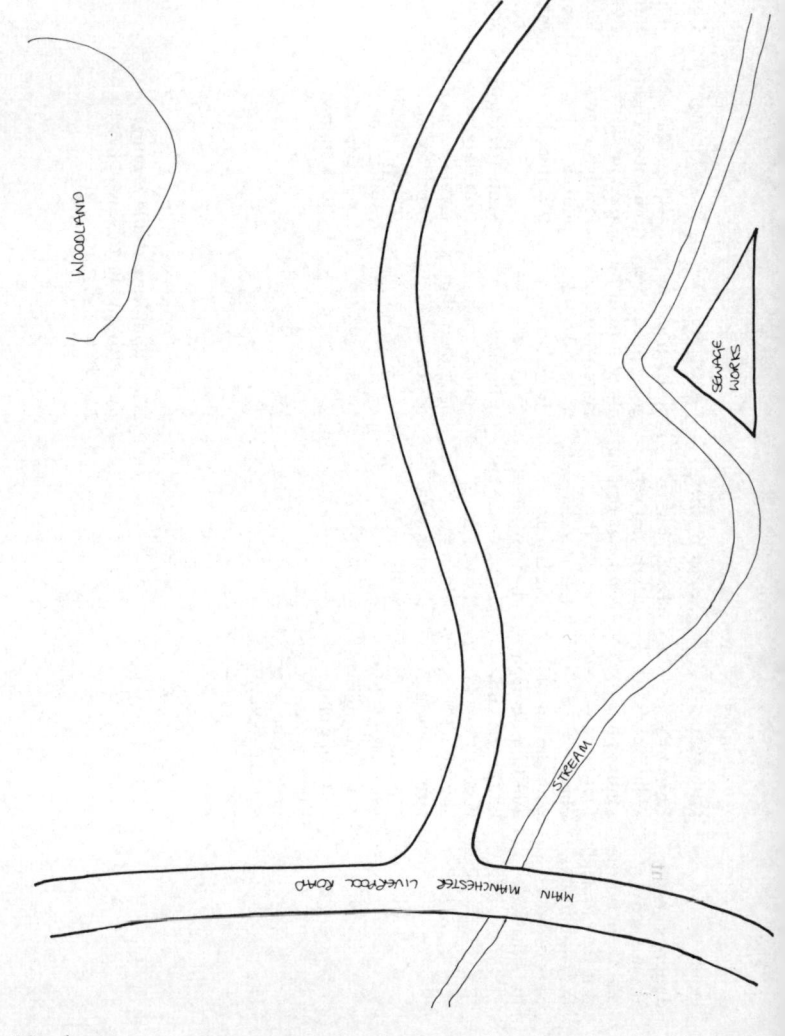

Map 1

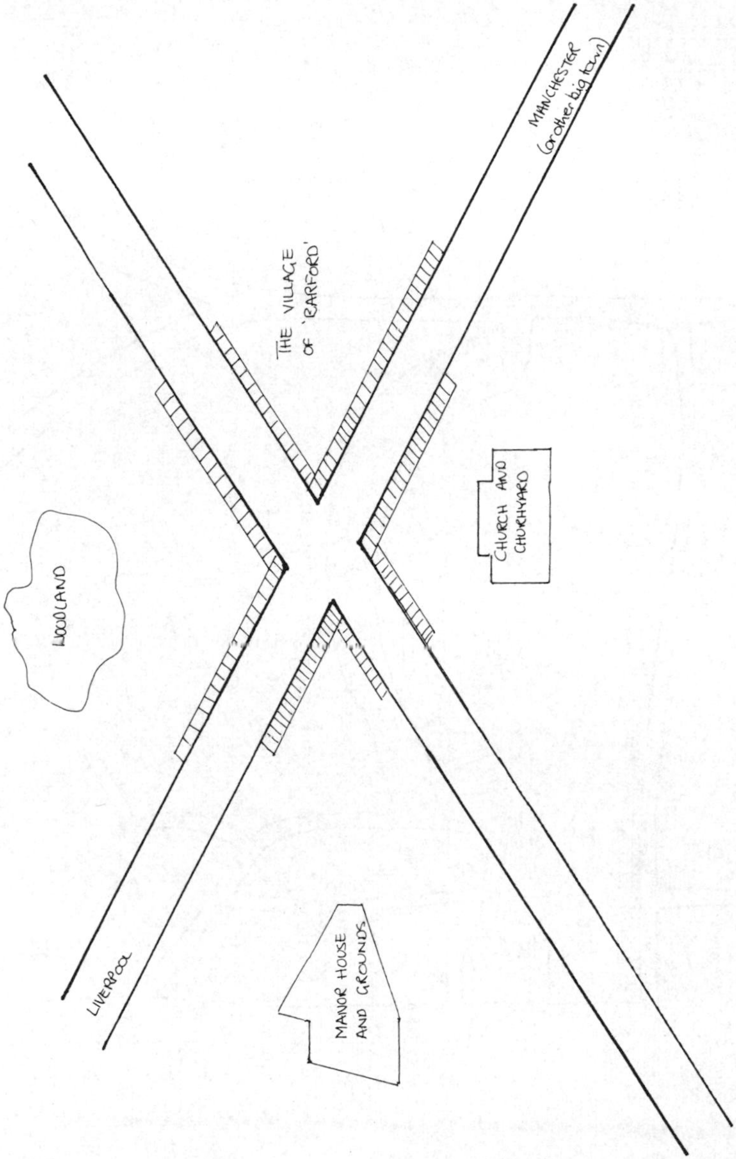

Map 2

MANOR HOUSE AND GROUNDS

LIVERPOOL

WOODLAND

CHURCH AND CHURCHYARD

THE VILLAGE OF 'EARFORD'

MANCHESTER (another big town)

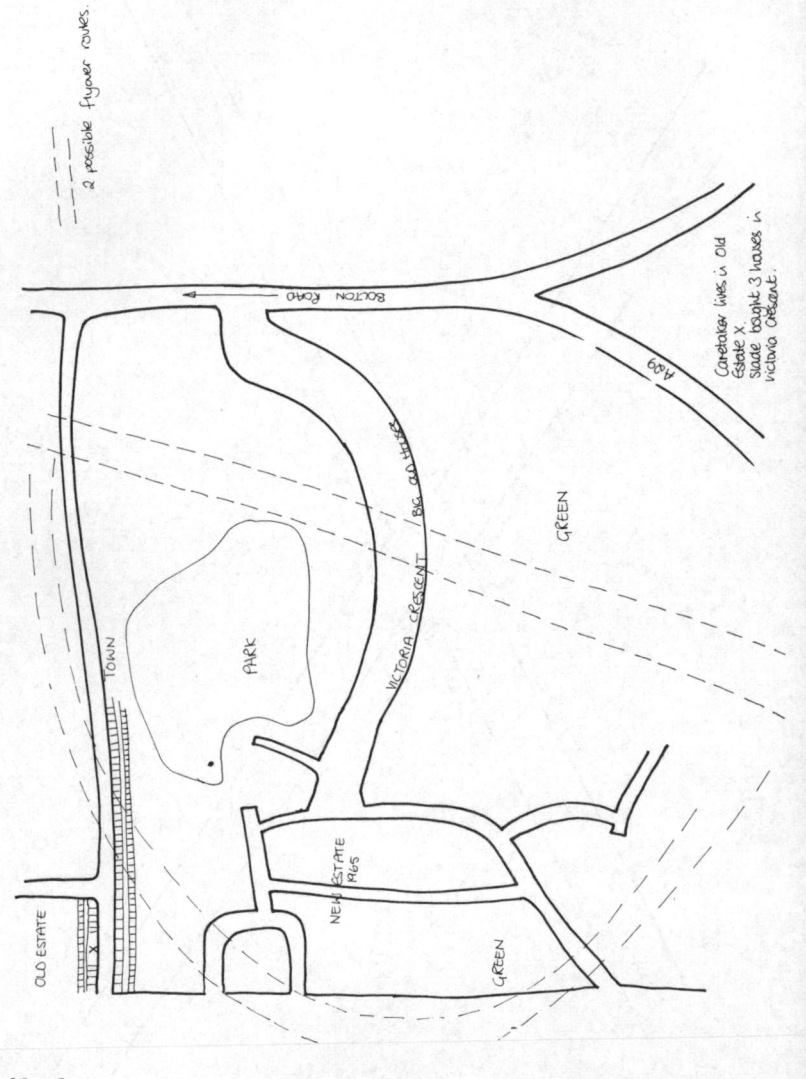

Map 3

3.35-4pm

The Social Worker and Caretaker then step out of role and discuss with the Pupils the implications of the events they have just witnessed. They clarify the fictitious nature of the programme for those still in doubt, but point out its accuracy and its relevance to them as future citizens. There is discussion about what the Caretaker could have done to make sure his case was heard and pupils are encouraged to think about different forms of concerted action which are available as means of opposing unacceptable decisions. The programme was originally performed at the height of the John Poulson scandal when talk about local government corruption was highly topical and pupils were able to relate the fictitious event they had witnessed to daily press coverage.

FACTORY

A Simulation Exercise

Devised by Rosemary Linnell for
The Curtain Theatre, London E1.

Introduction

What is a simulation? It is a way of setting up a collection of circumstances that will be as near to reality as possible, whilst still retaining the safeguards of a manufactured or unreal situation.

There is nothing new in this approach to education. Predatory animals use it in training their young in the techniques they will need when they have to face the real world; the armed forces have used simulation as a method of training for many years. Constantin Stanislavski used it to train actors.

It may be said that a full-scale simulation exercise, where even the physical surroundings are as accurate as possible comes somewhere between book learning and learning-on-the-job in providing a way of extending understanding, testing oneself and experimenting with circumstances under a controlled situation. It is not quite the same thing as a simulation 'game' where the physical surroundings are not included, nor is the learning process purely rational nor academic as in some published simulations since, by using actors in key roles, a human element is provided which can be either supportive, abrasive or challenging as situations or participants decide. 'Learning' under these circumstances may be emotional, and may not even be recognised as having taken place at all, until the simulated, or pretend situation is, later, compared with reality.

Such a powerful form of participation has obviously to be used with care, since, for those taking part, who may never have done any 'drama', theatricality and reality are not clearly separated. It is very important that whoever sets up the exercise remains reasonably sure of their educational objectives, can calculate potential response and, above all, that the actors can be confident enough and sensitive enough to play a supporting part without ever forcing an issue or determining an outcome, either for their own satisfaction, or in order to supply a 'right answer.'

It is because of this desirable absence of script, that it becomes very difficult to determine how to write down what goes on. The Curtain Theatre has set up three major simulations since 1974 when *Factory* was first performed. In 1976 *Steppington Dock* was evolved to deal with the subject of individual participation in local government. In 1978 *For Your Benefit* provided young people, working in role as trainee social-workers, with the opportunity of meeting some of the clients of the Welfare State and, by using the system as it stands, trying to bring the two together. The use of actors to play these problem people and an utterly realistic flat for them to live in provided an emotional and exhausting day for every student who took part. So taxing was this idea, for the actors, that two different problem families were created so that they could be alternated and thus prevent over-identification with the characters. It would be virtually impossible to re-create *For Your Benefit* in exactly the same way, but in 1979 it was feasible to consider repeating *Factory* and it so happened that at the very same moment the Torch Theatre in Milford Haven were looking for something to introduce T.I.E. into their work in the community, so it became important to try to make *Factory* accessible to others. What follows, then, is a summary of how the exercise was prepared and a running 'time-table' or scenario followed by some of the variables that could occur.

Curtain Theatre – London 1974

Preparation

After a while, working on simulations such as these, it becomes obvious that if you are aiming at near-reality, within which participants can make their own decisions, then everyone who is responsible needs to know everything that the real person, in a real situation, would know. In the case of *Factory,* the initial research was spread over a two-year span, during which time a number of small firms opened their doors to us, allowing surprisingly free access to their business and production methods. Based on these visits a 'profile' of the firm that would best serve our purpose was built up. We were not concerned just to give an idea of what it would be like to work in a factory, but to include an appropriate number of problem-solving exercises so that the young people might have the opportunity of experimenting with solutions and trying out ideas. It was for this reason that the firm we finally created had a specific history and therefore a specific present, which could produce a problematic future.

The Background Story

The firm was called 'East End Novelties Ltd.' Founded by Mr Bracht when he emigrated in the 1930s to England from Middle Europe, this family business began with a warehouse and a stall in Petticoat Lane, selling holy statues of garish plasterwork which were imported from his homeland. As Petticoat Lane is in the heart of what was a largely Jewish area, the Catholic images did not do as well as they might, so Bracht switched to other small objects such as would serve as prizes in a fairground; nick-nacks of all sorts, often imported, but sometimes copied in this country from eastern originals. He opened a shop nearby and began to manufacture more novelties. At the present time the workshop-cum-factory supplies other wholesalers and no longer has its own outlets. The only one of the original Bracht family is an aged director Bel'a Bracht, and as the programme opens, the firm has appointed a new, young managing director to carry on East End Novelties. From here on it is new territory and capable of taking many directions.

Building a Reality

It was fairly certain that, having invented a totally fictitious family firm,
the situation that the youngsters would find when they came to the
theatre should be far from perfect, otherwise there would be no
problems to solve. Our researches had sorted out those areas which in
reality provided management and workers with the most difficulty and
there were a great many other learning-areas which we wanted to
include. We intended to offer this programme to teachers who might
use it in connection with a study of 'work' in as wide a context as could
be imagined. We also thought that it might be especially appropriate to
the non-examination school-leavers, who could possibly find themselves
involved, in real life, in similar situations to our dramatic one. This made
it important that, in this programme anyway, we did not use a symbolic
or over-theatrical method which would only have alienated the young
people taking part. If we wanted them to believe totally in the situation
and their surroundings and take the issues seriously, then so must we.
We decided to build up our own characters by preparing all the material
needed, individually, so that, for example, the foreman was so
thoroughly conversant with the product being made that he knew every
last detail of manufacture and had cut, ruffled, pressed and packed
himself, had worked out hourly-rates and piece-rates with the shop
steward, had designed the production line and explained its
idiosyncrasies to the sales manager long before the programme opened.
This kind of detail allowed us to be fairly flexible in dealing with any
variants that the young people might want to put in and to deal
realistically with any question. It also helped to get inside the character,
which otherwise is difficult when you do not have either a script or any
way of rehearsing.

This was particularly important when the programme was repeated in
1979, with a different cast, as the preparation time was only four days.

It was decided that the areas to be explored were mainly those of
management/worker relationships and conditions of work, which latter
included fundamental questions about why people work at all, and what
is important to them in a work situation. We then began to create the
factory premises.

Building an Environment

We used the Theatre itself to provide us with an entrance lobby with
wide stairs up to the first floor suite of offices, wood-panelled and
impressive. Here were desks, coat racks, drawing equipment,
typewriters, a telephone and a boardroom table. The lavatories on this
floor are large and reasonably fitted out, the windows admit plenty of
light. It is warm. Across a wet alleyway from the same lobby is the fire
exit at the back of the stage area. Downstairs in the basement is our own
theatre workshop and two dressing rooms which were converted to
locker rooms and a scruffy, windowless 'rest room' where tea was
brewed. The lavatories on this floor are dark and unpleasant. On ground
level the stage was transformed. A wall of depressing greyness was

built across the proscenium opening; the stripped-down stage looked like
a huge barn. Strip lights hung over a connected system of trestle tables.
Cardboard boxes spilled pieces of cloth all over the place. It is clean but
depressing. Without the normal warmth of curtains the scene-dock door
admits fierce draughts; by the entrance door a time-clock was fitted.
There are back stairs which lead to the offices above. All the labels on
the theatre's doors were covered with the factory's labels; 'Musak' was
piped from a remote source on to the shop floor.

Building the Action

The schools were asked to send a complete work-force of about forty
young people in answer to a series of job 'ads' that we sent out. These
were based on the going rates for the job, and ranged from the
managing director with a yearly salary through accounts and sales staff,
designers (a slot for shyer, less forthcoming students), secretarial
assistants, despatch clerks and store keeper, mostly on weekly and
monthly salaries, to the piece-workers on the shop floor. Teachers were
to be quality controllers or rate fixers. The preparation was left entirely
to the teachers, provided that they brought their pupils prepared to go
to work. We asked that they should be allowed to come 'suitably
dressed.' Many teachers held interviews and included the writing of job
letters in their preparation. Some of them also spent time on the
different payment schemes, training potential and so on.

Meanwhile, the actors prepared themselves. We cast a managing
director's secretary, or personal assistant, smooth, efficient and
deferential; a sales manager, impetuous, dynamic, persuasive; a designer,
concerned largely with providing the necessary artefacts for the firm; a
foreman, traditional, also efficient, quite a fatherly figure; the storeman,
who was also the shop steward of the T.G.W.U.; a telephonist, who was
also the stage manager of the piece and provided all 'voices off' on a
specially installed phone system. There were also extra characters
involved, for example we either had a Factories Inspector (Curtain 1979.)
or used the Health and Safety at Work Act to introduce a small
skirmish about responsibility for safety. This was either fed in by the
caretaker (Torch Theatre 1979) or by the shop steward (1979) Curtain.)
There were also roles for visitors and an ubiquitous tea-lady (the director)
who kept an eye on things.

Most of the rehearsal period was spent in preparing to take on our young
assistants; every small thing that they might need to know, in any
forseeable eventuality, had to be provided. Because of this, it had been
decided that one person (the director) should draw up the timetable
(see below) which was our only 'script'; everyone else worked on their
own preparation, combining when necessary so that everything tied up
and there were no discrepencies (other than deliberate imbalances, for
example in the number of skilled and unskilled jobs.) We then 'talked
through' the day's activities which were scheduled to begin at 10 am and
end whenever the class was ready to finish, i.e. had arrived at some kind
of solution, which was likely to be around 3 pm. Large sections of this
timetable were impossible to fill in, others were carefully placed to
coincide with each other, such as the break for lunch or the timing of
phone calls.

Rehearsals were also notable for the welcome visits from such people as
trade unionists, who were able to help in a number of ways, particularly
in listening to the actors talking through their contribution to the
exercise and then commenting on or correcting us on attitudes and facts.
Without this sort of check we would have been seriously handicapped in
our intention of absolute reality.

The Timetable – Curtain Theatre

10.00 Kids arrive. Met by Stage Manager and introduced to the idea of inventing a background for themselves and that they will be asked to think of themselves as adult workers. Badges, to coincide with numbers on time-clock, issued to shop floor workers, this also serves as a check on roles.

10.5 Secretary greets Managing Director by name - Mr or Miss: takes office staff away to hang up coats and generally settle in.

10.10 Foreman leads everyone else through yard to locker rooms and then to clock in.

10.15 New office staff have met the older members of the staff. Two sales assistants and two accounts clerks are given files with portions of the month's figures in each. Added together they give a total picture of income and outgoings. They are helped to understand the firms' status and asked to prepare to give a report at the monthly report meeting which will happen at about 11.00 am. Managing Director is taken through minutes of last meeting and agenda for this one. Design assistants lay out and make tracings of working drawings for new product (a do-it-yourself kit) thereby learning all its components.

Clocking-in at East End Novelties.

Secretary takes orders for coffee and lets S.M. know so that she can make it.

10.20 Foreman and Storekeeper show each worker on the shop floor where to work. Foreman demonstrates the finished product, a clown made to dangle in a car window and explains how each process follows on the other, to the moment it is packed up and despatched. Teachers given clip-boards and stop-watches to help in instructing individuals, according to cards affixed to workplaces, which also set out piece-rates. Storekeeper also helps in these processes and talks to workers about joining union. Comes round to enrol members.

10.45 Office staff assemble around large table for meeting. Coffee and biscuits. Managing Director slowly finds his or her feet in chairing meeting and hearing reports. After run-down on state of firm's financial situation from kids, Sales Manager does a punchy report on how well the firm's stand at DIY Exhibition had done and how new orders were expected. Design assistants explain new product. On pre-arranged signal phone rings. It is a buyer from Fullworths. Large order will be placed if delivery date can be met. Due to wobbly finances and virtual end of 'clown' orders this phone call is met with definite optimism.

The foreman instructs skilled workers in their trade.

11.00 Shop floor workers, having settled down to their work and having either joined the union, or not, as the individual case might be, have a first break. They troop down to scruffy but warm room in basement. Usually light cigarettes in defiance of teachers. Tea in battered mugs. No proper ventilation. Hazards apparent, but if not discussed by kids, Health and Safety Act invoked by shop steward (storekeeper.) He's asked to raise issue with the management, enlists support of kids. On return to shop floor other complaints about conditions raised, notably unsafe condition of pressing equipment (iron - actually this is faked but it looks bad.) also packing material which lies all across fire-door. Small dispute between foreman and shop steward about presser who will lose job and therefore cash. New place for iron found. Electric fire will have to be unplugged. It is not very warm. Thermometer fetched. Complaints listed with help of shop steward. Kids usually feel riled about 'Musak' and lavatories and the quality of the scissors they have to use. Some way found to convey complaints 'upstairs' (note, phone call, deputation).

11.35 (approx.) In the office the questions are piling up, about how the new DIY product will be made. Samples of cloth are called for, by a phone call to the assistant storekeeper from a design assistant. (Both the callers are kids, so this is a keeping-a-straight-face situation.) Two kids off shop floor are sent up with samples of cloth in stock. This allows two 'spies' unintentionally to overhear details of new product, which should serve as alarm signal to others on shop floor. No assembly in factory means loss of all skilled jobs. Will kids understand implications of what they see and hear? On their return they are asked what samples

The shop floor at East End Novelties.

were for and what was going on, but no pressure is used to extract information. Phone calls are made from various departments to 'outside' firms (each one is put through 'switchboard' and 'connected' to place requested. Many of these calls have to be improvised by stage manager as they vary so much but mostly information is requested on prices of materials, advertising and printing.) One call goes to foreman, as chief designer requests tables being shifted because of poor light. Will a couple of hands come and move tables? After certain aggravation, foreman brings two more 'spies' with him and, by moving desks, details of design are clearly visible to shop floor workers. Also conditions of work 'upstairs' are seen by workers from 'downstairs' and can be used as a reference later. At this point also, a memo, ordering workers to take tea in the canteen in future is issued (canteen is theatre coffee bar where prices are displayed and are considerably more than 'free' tea in basement) to meet safety regulations.

12.15 (approx.) The Managing Director has to meet first real tests, 'Robinsons' have to be informed that the last few hundred of their 'clown' order cannot be completed, yet East End Novelties need payment for all those which have been delivered so far. A difficult job for a fifteen-year-old boy or girl, especially as 'Robinsons' can be quite difficult if not handled right.

Rumours on the shop floor are probably buzzing by the time some of the sales staff, accountants and designers (or some of them) go down to the shop floor to announce that this delightful, new DIY product will be put into manufacture this afternoon. A layout of the process involved in making it is left with the foreman, but before any discussion can get underway the foreman rings the electric bell for lunch.

Managing Director for a day.

12.30 They clock out and leave the factory floor. Office workers also go to lunch.

N.B. In 1974 lunch hour was also part of the exercise; which proved of immense value to the kids and included a showing of a BBC film 'Member of the Union', but for the actors it was an enormous strain and in 1979 lunch was 'time off' for everyone.

1.30 Resumption of work. Whether office or shop floor workers a few quiet minutes are taken to settle back into their roles and to resume concentration, then the pace quickens because the office personnel have finished their immediate rush. The new product is settled. It has been put through all the necessary processes and the meeting which was adjourned in the morning (to allow the new product to be assessed in terms of the number of hours overtime it would require to complete the order by the required deadline, the changes in the piece rate and the cost of re-stocking materials. etc) is resumed, and the next item on the agenda is dealt with. This is the firm's annual dinner-dance, two of the meeker assistants from the office are asked to go down to the shop-floor and find out how many people want tickets; they arrive at the height of what has been happening on the shop-floor. The foreman has asked for all work on the clown to stop and describes to the work-force exactly what is involved in the new product. The major change is that whereas there were a number of skilled jobs at a higher rate of pay, on the new DIY product there are no assemblers, no pressers, no rufflers, no finishers etc. there are only markers, cutters and packers required.

At this point there is usually no need for anyone to point out to the young people what this involves, usually it is enough for the shop steward to help to focus their natural dissatisfactions and for him to take whatever steps are needed to help the pupils to organise some sort of protest. It is usual for the shop steward to phone the union local office, to ask for their advice and then circumstances determine whether a union meeting is called for those who have joined or some other method is found for negotiating with management. The presence of two office workers at the height of this hullaballoo is noted and the foreman keeps them hanging about until he can deal with them. After they've heard enough to realise what is going on he sends them away, without answering their question. They have inadvertantly acted as spies and on their return to the office will report that work has ceased and the work-force are holding a meeting.

What happens after this point is variable, but after each group has had a chance of clarifying their own position as to how much the firm can afford to pay and how much the piece workers want (in money and improved conditions) then the actors try to ensure that the entire staff meet on the shop floor for a final settlement.

Depending on the young people's stamina and the terms which they wish to negotiate the afternoon may last 1½ - 2 hours and be rounded off with a simple running down and returning to reality, or with questions. No serious or deep discussion is entered into at this point, partly because most of the day has been spent in this way partly because the teachers' involvement has been constant throughout the day and they may want to continue using the programme as a common reference point without feeling that all the potential has been squeezed from it in one go.

Variations

The Torch Theatre, Milford Haven 1979

The Arts Council of Wales funded a short season of *Factory* at the Torch Theatre as an introduction to educational theatre in their work in the community. The high level of unemployment in the area and the recent efforts being made to open small workshops and factories and to encourage tourism, gave the company a variant on the original scenario.

Crair Craft (a bastard Welsh-English name, implying keepsakes, heirlooms or relics) was supposedly set up by the Welsh Development Board to provide alternative work in the area. Their first 'line' was a collage pack, of genuine, cut-out pieces of traditional fabric, attached to a card labelled 'Blodwen, the lucky Welsh doll'. It was so obviously a low-standard object that when the Development Board complained that this was not really a craft product, the move to a new and a highly skilled second line, was the lifeline the firm needed to maintain development grants and increase profits. The problems caused by this particular changeover are obviously strikingly different from the original. In this case, it is all highly skilled work, slow and not amenable to the same pay structure. The young people have to look for different solutions in the structuring of the work process and the establishment of a basic wage, but nevertheless the negotiating requires a similar level of skill if an acceptable solution is to be found.

The timing and structure of the programme was almost exactly similar in all other respects and the preparation was carried out in an identical way, although inevitably the actors' roles varied according to their own personalities.

Other variations took place within all three versions of *Factory*. Every day was totally different, not just in the pupils' response but in their method of working out problems and in the eventual solutions which they arrived at. Because of this variability, it is not possible to suggest a fixed script by which readers may be able to reproduce the actors' roles exactly but the formula may be applied to a number of different circumstances where important issues are 'discovered' by the young people concerned and where 'negotiation' is required to resolve their difficulties. Although the amount of information contained in such a programme is quite large, each pupil will begin by only handling a small account, until a growth in confidence enables more and more responsibility to be taken on by those capable of handling it.